D1564587

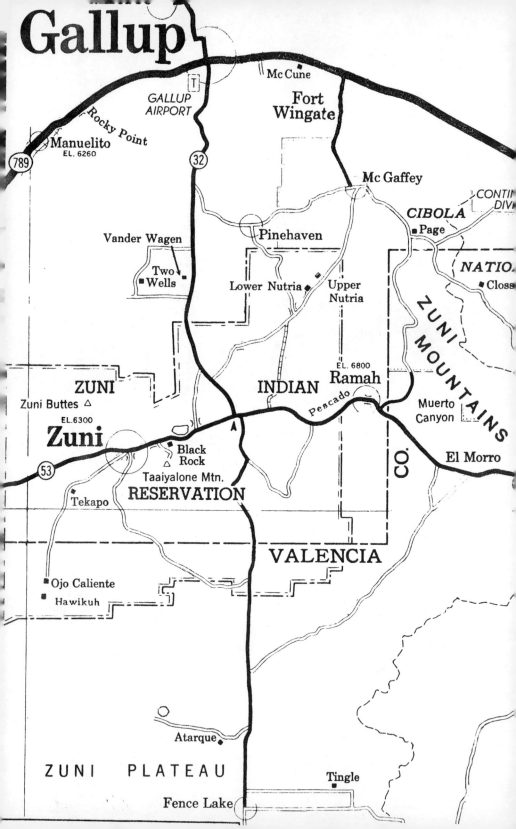

dorothea c. leighton
john adair

people of the
middle place

a study of the zuni indians

BEHAVIOR SCIENCE MONOGRAPHS

First printing, 1966
Second printing, 1971

ISBN 0-87536-320-2
Library of Congress Catalog Card Number: 65-28463

Manufactured in the United States of America

To Laura Thompson
and Dorothy Jones Adair
with deep appreciation

This book is the last of a series of tribal monographs reporting the results of the Indian Education Research Project, later called the Indian Education Personality and Administration Project. This endeavor was undertaken jointly in 1941 by the Committee on Human Development of the University of Chicago and the United States Office of Indian Affairs. The immediate objective of the project was to investigate, analyze, and compare the development of personality in five Indian tribes in the context of their total environment--sociocultural, geographical, and historical--for implications related to Indian Service Administration. The long-range research aim was to evaluate the whole Indian administrative program, with special reference to the effect of present policy on individuals, to indicate the direction toward which this policy was leading, and to suggest how the effectiveness of Indian administration might be increased.

The other tribal monographs already published are: The Hopi Way by Laura Thompson and Alice Joseph (University of Chicago Press, 1944), Warriors without Weapons by Gordon Macgregor (University of Chicago Press, 1946), The Navaho and Children of The People by Clyde Kluckhohn and Dorothea Leighton (Harvard University Press, 1946 and 1947), and The Desert People by Alice Joseph, Rosamond Spicer, and Jane Chesky (University of Chicago Press, 1949). The final report of the Project, Personality and Government by Laura Thompson, was published in 1951 by the Instituto Indigenista Interamericano, Mexico, D. F.

It will be noted that a considerable time has elapsed between the last tribal monograph and the present one. The reason for this lies partly in the difficulty experienced in finding anyone who was well acquainted with Zuni and who still had time and inclination to write the kind of tribal description that would be helpful in understanding the implications of the research findings. Eventually John Adair was persuaded to undertake the task. He had not been present at Zuni at the time the testing program of the Project was being conducted, and his own studies there in 1947-48 were focused on the effect of the returned veterans of World War II on the pueblo and vice versa. Although he had little need or opportunity in this work to collect material on child development, he was fortunate to have access to the unpublished notes on child behavior and child rearing practices which Dr. Omer C. Stewart had made during his researches at Zuni in 1940-41. From his study of the veterans, however, he acquired some understanding of adult Zuni personality and of what Zuni culture means to the Zuni.

For the rest of Part I he has drawn principally on previously published accounts of Zuni religious, social, and economic life, both ancient and modern. He has conferred also with Zuni experts and with Indian Service officials who have worked at Zuni. From these sources he has put together a description of life at Zuni which is not intended to be exhaustive but rather to form a background of understanding of the cultural whole against which the results of the testing program of the Zuni children can be projected. For the reader's orientation: Part I was written by John Adair, while Part II is by Dorothea Leighton. Chapter 13, "The Changing Pueblo," was written by Adair, and certain revisions were added by Leighton.

Publisher's Note

The material for this tribal monograph, PEOPLE OF THE MIDDLE PLACE: A Study of the Zuni Indians, was generously made available to the Human Relations Area Files by the authors, Dorothea C. Leighton and John Adair. First processed and placed in the Files in 1963, it is now being issued by HRAF Press for general distribution, thus completing publication of the series of six integrative studies of Indian personality which were produced as part of the Indian Education Research Project.

ACKNOWLEDGMENTS

As is the case with any book written by more than one person, the two authors have utilized the aid of various people in collecting and arranging the materials of this volume. However, we have certain shared indebtednesses. The first of these is to the Zuni themselves--more especially the veterans for Part I and the children for Part II, but also to all other Zuni, both past and present, who have allowed anthropologists to stay with them and study their way of life.

Next we are grateful for all the help provided by the Indian Service staff, both at Zuni and at the United Pueblos Agency in Albuquerque. Without this active assistance of many staff members, our work would have been impossible. The list below will name all the individuals involved. Here we would like to single out Mr. and Mrs. Gonzales, who have lived with the Zuni for many years, and the two Indian Office superintendents in charge during our periods of work there, Mr. Walter Olson and Mr. Robert Bunker. It is difficult to express adequately our thanks for the many kindnesses as well as for the valuable information supplied by these people. Without Mrs. Gonzales' devotion and persistence against great odds, the testing program would have died, half done. Behind these more immediate participants stood the staff of the Indian Office itself, encouraging and facilitating our work in many ways, both during the testing and afterward.

Dr. Leighton is obliged to the Social Science Research Council and the John Simon Guggenheim Memorial Foundation for fellowships which made her work in anthropology possible, and equally to the late Dr. Adolf Meyer and his successor, Dr. John C. Whithorn, of the Phipps Psychiatric Clinic at Johns Hopkins Hospital, for arranging for her to pursue this work.

Dr. Adair also is the recipient of fellowship aid from the Social Science Research Council. He would like to thank particularly Mr. and Mrs. Robert Bunker and Mr. and Mrs. Marcel Weinrich, for help in preparing the manuscript, and Mr. Clifford Barnett for important editorial aid.

For increasing his understanding of the Zuni and their ways, he would like to thank Dr. Evon Vogt, who did a parallel study of Navaho veterans, Dr. Clyde Kluckhohn, who advised on many matters, Dr. Bert Kaplan, who helped in interpreting life history materials, and Dr. George Mills, who provided information on life at Ojo Caliente. Special thanks are due Dr. Omer C. Stewart, whose unpublished notes on Zuni children form the basis for much of Chapter 7.

We are both indebted to Dr. Alexander H. Leighton, who released us from other obligations from time to time in order to work on this volume. He and a number of others have read the manuscript in part or in whole and offered valuable suggestions in regard both to form and content. Other critics are Dr. John Roberts, Dr. Evon Vogt, Dr. Esther Goldfrank Wittfogel, Dr. Laura Thompson, and Dr. Florence Hawley Ellis.

It is not possible to list all the individuals who have influenced us in our outlook and interpretation of human facts, but we wish to acknowledge a general indebtedness to our many teachers and associates, whose thoughts are inextricably mixed with our own.

D.C.L.

J.A.

INDIAN EDUCATION RESEARCH STAFF

Committee on Indian Education Research

University of Chicago

Office of Indian Affairs

W. Lloyd Warner, chairman
Robert J. Havighurst
Ralph Tyler

John Collier, chairman
Willard W. Beatty
Rene d'Harnoncourt
Joseph McCaskill

Laura Thompson, coordinator

Zuni Project Staff

Field Workers

Richard Birnbaum, M.D.
Marie Deatherage
Kathleen Erickson
Christine Garcia
Clara Gonzales
H. W. Gratton
Willene Griffin

Helene Higgins
Josephine Howard
Ethel Lane
Dorothea Leighton, M.D.
Leonard Otipoby
Evelyn Page

Test Analysts

Free Drawings

Rorschach

Thematic Apperception

Lisbeth Eubank
Brooke Mordy

Dorothea Leighton

William E. Henry

(Under the Supervision of R. J. Havighurst)

<u>Emotional Response</u>	<u>Moral Ideology</u>
Jean Hall	Jeanette Murstine
Iva O. Schmidt	
<u>Arthur Performance</u>	<u>Goodenough Draw-a-Man</u>
Rhea R. Hilkevitch	Minna K. Gunther
	Inez E. Pratt

Advisory Committee

Grace Arthur	Bruno Klopfer
Ruth Benedict	Clyde Kluckhohn
Allison Davis	Eugene Lerner
Fred Eggan	Kurt Lewin
Erik Erikson	D'Arcy McNickle
Lawrence Frank	Margaret Mead
A. Irving Hallowell	Scudder Mekeel

TABLE OF CONTENTS

List of Photographs   xiv
List of Tables   xv

Part I: Zuni Life Today and Yesterday   1

  Introduction   1

  Chapter 1 The Pueblo and the People   4

      The Land of the People   4
      The Climate   5
      Population   6
      Physical Type and Dress   6
      Language   8
      Modernization   9

  Chapter 2 Zuni History   11

      The Mythological Account   11
      The Archaeological Record   13
      The Conquest by Spain   15
      Early Missions   18
      Later Missions   19
      Changes Wrought   20
      Relations with the United States Government   22

  Chapter 3 Farmers, Herders, and Silversmiths   23

      Early Innovations   23
      Trading Posts   24

The Growth of Silvercraft   25
Irrigation   26
Farm Extension   27
Livestock   30
  Division of labor and ownership   30
  Sheep management   31
  Stock reduction   32
Tribal Income   33
The Changing Economy   34

Chapter 4 Clan and Kin   39

The Clan Today   39
Kinship   42
Social Change   43

Chapter 5 Religion   45

Purposes and Functions   45
Religious Techniques   47
Structure of Religious Groupings   48
Religious Change   52

Chapter 6 Civil Government: The Separation of State
from Church   55

Chapter 7 Life Cycle   60

Pregnancy and Childbirth   60
Infancy and Early Childhood   62
Later Childhood   66
Adolescence and Marriage   74
Death Customs   78

Part II: A Testing Program at Zuni   80

Introduction   80
  Interview and background material   80
  Health examinations   81
  Intelligence tests   81
  The psychological battery   81
  The projective tests   82

Analysis of Tests   83
Selection of Subjects   84

Chapter 8 Intelligence of Zuni Children   87

Sex Differences   90

Chapter 9 Health of Zuni Children   91

Chapter 10 The Psychological Battery   95

The Emotional Response Test   96
Themes of responses   102
Personal relationships   104
Bavelas Moral Ideology Test   107
Immanent Justice and Animism   111
Attitude of Zuni Children toward Rules of Games 112

Chapter 11 The Projective Tests   115

Free Drawings   115
Thematic Apperception Test   117
Rorschach Test   119

Chapter 12 "The Zuni Child" and Zuni Children 122

Amy   124
Charles   126
Clara   127
Peter   130
Angela   132
Frank   135

Chapter 13 The Changing Pueblo — Conclusions
and Expectations   139

Footnotes   145

Bibliography   151

Index   161

LIST OF PHOTOGRAPHS

1. The old terraced pueblo, about 1897 (Ben Wittick Collection)

2. Aerial view of Zuni, 1947 (Harvey Caplin)

3. Zuni pueblo with Toyallene, the sacred mesa, in the background (U. S. Indian Service)

4. Zuni and Toyallene in winter (Adair)

5. The central dance plaza (U. S. Indian Service)

6. The old church in the late nineteenth century (Ben Wittick Collection)

7. An ancient spring (U. S. Indian Service)

8. A vegetable garden (U. S. Indian Service)

9. Building an oven (Adair)

10. Bread dough is prepared in large quantities (U. S. Indian Service)

11. Baking bread for several families (U. S. Indian Service)

12. Enough dough for an oven-full (U. S. Indian Service)

13. A full oven (U. S. Indian Service)

14. Some of the grazing land is bare and eroded (Adair)

15. Lambs penned for selling (Adair)

16. Splitting firewood (U. S. Indian Service)

17. Drawing water from the village well (U. S. Indian Service)

18. Silversmith carving a rock mold (Adair)

19. Grinding corn in the ancient way with metate and mano (U. S. Indian Service)

20. An old Zuni potter, 1940 (U. S. Indian Service)

21. A woman silversmith (U. S. Indian Service)

22. Men in black blankets, 1940 (United Pueblos Agency)

23. Schoolgirls with shawls (U. S. Indian Service)

24. Zuni schoolgirls (U. S. Indian Service)

25. Ready for a ceremonial dance (U. S. Indian Service)

26. A middle-aged woman (Adair)

27. An old woman of the Badger clan (Adair)

28. A Zuni housewife (Adair)

29. A Zuni woman with her basket of ceremonial cornmeal (U. S. Indian Service)

30. A fortune in turquoise (Adair)

31. A young Zuni couple (U. S. Indian Service)

LIST OF TABLES

Table	I	Number of Acres Harvested per Crop	29
Table	II	Breakdown of Total Income from Sales of Agricultural and Livestock Products	30
Table	III	Age and Sex Distribution of Zuni Children Tested	85
Table	IV	Age Range, Sex Distribution, and Total Number of Subjects for Various Tests	86
Table	V	School Enrollment of Zuni Children 6-18 Years Old, 1942-43	88
Table	VI	Distribution of IQ's Earned on the Arthur and Goodenough Tests	89
Table	VII	Sex Differences	90
Table	VIII	Percentages of the 97 Sample Children, Showing Various Health Conditions by Group, Sex, and Age Level	93

Table   IX   Average Number of Responses to the Emo-
                tional Response Test   96

Table   X   Differences in Reaction of Zuni Boys and Girls
                to the Emotional Response Test: Happiness   97

Table   XI   Differences in Reaction of Zuni Boys and Girls
                to the Emotional Response Test: Sadness   98

Table   XII   Differences in Reaction of Zuni Boys and Girls
                to the Emotional Response Test: Fear   99

Table   XIII Differences in Reaction of Zuni Boys and Girls
                to the Emotional Response Test: Anger   100

Table   XIV   Differences in Reaction of Zuni Boys and Girls
                to the Emotional Response Test: Shame   101

Table   XV   Differences in Reaction of Zuni Boys and Girls
                to the Emotional Response Test: Best Thing   102

Table   XVI   Differences in Reaction of Zuni Boys and Girls
                to the Emotional Response Test: Worst Thing   102

Table   XVII Persons Involved in "Positive" and "Negative"
                Relationships to Zuni Children   105

Table   XVIII Categories of Moral Ideology Responses of
                Zuni and White Children   108

Table   XIX   Praisers and Blamers Mentioned by Zuni and
                White Children   110

Table   XX   Attitudes toward Rules of Games, by Age
                and Sex of Rule Changers   113

Table   XXI   Items in Free Drawings Showing Relative
                Influence of White and Native Cultures   116

Table   XXII Percentage of Items Showing White or Native
                Culture for the Six Indian Groups   117

PART I: ZUNI LIFE TODAY AND YESTERDAY

INTRODUCTION

As the tourist drives down to Zuni on the road leading south from Gallup, he finds himself descending from the plateau green with conifers. Ahead, high sandstone mesas loom abruptly from the floor of a wide valley. Far below, the Zuni river flows to the west. During most of the year it is a mere trickle of water, but that trickle has sustained the life of these people, who have built their main village and outlying hamlets along its course.

The road crosses the rocky stream bed and turns west, following the edge of the most massive of the mesas. High overhead, overlooking the valley, is an airplane beacon, a symbol of the modern technology which these people have come to accept. Turning from the southern horizon, mesa filled, to the other side of the road, the tourist sees first a compound of government buildings surrounded by a wall. As the road takes a final dip into the lower valley, he drives by some white buildings erected by the Civil Aeronautics Authority on the edge of the black escarpment.

Telephone and electric wires are strung beside the road that leads into the pueblo. The houses that have been built along this road are constructed of concrete blocks and have gabled roofs. The larger ones are made of red rock quarried from the nearby mesas, cut to a hard symmetry and mortised with cement. There is a curious mixture of new and old: several houses have Venetian blinds at the windows, while alongside are the beehive-shaped ovens where the women, even today, bake their bread. The road leads on past several trading posts, a post office, and a soft drink and snack bar from which a juke box blares.

The casual visitor may gain admittance to some of the houses and see the water now piped into a porcelain sink, no longer hauled from some distant spring on donkey back. He may visit one of the trading posts and see a self-service market designed for Indian customers. Autos are everywhere, driven by men dressed in levis. The women and girls wear cotton dresses, but cover their heads and shoulders with brightly colored shawls, which bear Czechoslovakian labels. The tourist who wanders around the village will see the ancient Catholic Mission, falling in ruin, roofless, and standing like some ancient monument, a relic of former days. The innermost part of the village surrounding the old church is built where the old terraced pueblo once stood, and has an architecture more traditional than that seen on the edge of town. All the houses have flat roofs and walls of rough-cut stone plastered over with adobe. The kivas (ceremonial chambers), so dramatic and imposing in the Rio Grande pueblos, here are simple, square structures, matching the architecture of the old houses, and marked only by long ladders which extend up from the roofs.

If the visitor addresses one of the villagers he is answered in English, spoken clearly yet timidly by the women, forcefully by the men. Conversation may lead to friendship, and may also convey the impression of a people well accustomed to the white man's way of life. The visitor to the village reasons: he lives like us, he talks like us, therefore he is like us.

But should the tourist climb to the top of the nearby mesa, just below the beacon, he may stumble upon an idol, the image of the War God, with offerings of meal, shell, and turqoise. It is then that he learns that the apparently friendly, outgoing Zuni are not as much like the white man as they at first appear. How can we account for this discrepancy--a modernized pueblo guarded by a War God?

Analysis of the people in this now modernized pueblo will reveal two forces. One, the force of the non-Zuni world pulling the individual outward, like some felt but unseen centrifugal force, ever whirling him away from the center. The other, an inward force which holds the individual strongly to the Middle Place (see Chapter 2). The outward force is best characterized simply as twentieth-century America--as the material culture that is ours, which is replacing theirs. Sometimes the individual loses hold and is thrown from the pueblo orbit to the outside world. This happens only when the second, inward force is cut off. That inward force, as we shall see, is the force of religion. It is essentially the belief system with its accompanying methods of social control that has held these people in one large main village for so many generations. The outward force is evident on first acquaintance with the village. The inward force becomes understood only through long association and study.

A magic circle is drawn by the pueblo around its inner core, and by each Zuni around his own center. No matter whether you are a tourist striking up a conversation with a passerby or a psychologist using projective techniques, sooner or later this barrier will be felt. Easy conversation will be replaced by chilly silence if the tourist should ask what takes place at the shrine on the mesa top.

This magic circle is not unique to Zuni; it exists to some extent in all the pueblos. But what is remarkable is the delicate balance of the inward and outward forces of resistance to and acceptance of change, which has allowed the Zuni to take on so many of our ways and still retain the essential core of their own values. Will this balance be maintained in the future? Or will the structure crack and crumble, as it has to a marked degree in such pueblos as Laguna, where appearance and inner reality are no longer separate entities?

CHAPTER 1

THE PUEBLO AND THE PEOPLE

The Land of the People

The reservation of the Zuni Indians is located in the southwestern corner of McKinley county in western New Mexico. Its area comprises 342,046
acres. The main village, Zuni Pueblo, is situated on the original land granted
to the Indians by the King of Spain in 1689, and occupied by them previous to
this from time immemorial. Twice during the nineteenth century and once
during the present century, major additions were made to the original Spanish
grant. In addition, in 1935 the Zuni were given certain use rights to grazing
lands administered by the Indian Service. Thus, as of 1943, the total land
used by the Zuni tribe comprised 414,982 acres.[1]
    The figure means little by itself. We should note that the Zuni reser-
vation is approximately two-thirds the size of the Hopi land use area, and that
while the acreage per capita of the two areas is comparable, their worth as
farming and range land is not, since the Zuni land is of much better quality
and is better watered than that of the Hopi. Furthermore, the Zuni have 2,833
acres of land under irrigation, while the Hopi have only a fraction of that
amount.
    The reservation is on the southeastern edge of the Colorado plateau.
This is high, rugged country, with an average elevation of 7,100 feet. The
highest area is at the northeast corner of the reservation, which slopes off from
the Zuni mountains, where, at an altitude of 9,000 feet, these mountains form
part of the Continental Divide. The land slopes to the southwest, thus deter-
mining the course of the Zuni river and its main tributary, Nutria Creek. The
irregular edge of the plateau that abuts off from the Zuni mountains forms the
sides of the mesas rising up on the north and the south above the broad valley,
which has been eroded away from the original tableland.[2]

A disconnected section of this plateau rises a sheer thousand feet above the valley floor to form the sacred mesa, Toyallane, known to white residents both as Corn Mountain and Thunder Mountain. On the north are two smaller mesas of comparable height called Kwilliyallane. These mesas and two buttes to the west enclose the Zuni valley on all sides of the horizon except in the southwest, where the land flattens into a broad plain.

Along the water courses flowing from the Zuni mountains lie the various farming villages, starting with Nutria in the northeast, on the banks of the creek of that name. South and west of Nutria is Pescado, a little to the west of Ramah, the Mormon town that is just over the reservation line. At Pescado several large springs gush from under an old lava bed to join the Rio Nutria. Near Black Rock, the government establishment, the waters from both creeks are impounded behind a dam installed by the government in 1909 to irrigate the lower valley. The irrigation ditch first courses along the north side of the valley, with laterals leading off from it to the fields that surround the main pueblo.

Beyond Black Rock, the combined Rio Pescado and Rio Nutria flow southwest to add their confluence to other streams to form the Zuni river, just above the village. Down-river from Zuni is the smallest of the farming villages, Tekapa, or Hill Ranch, situated on a rise to the side of the road that leads further south and west to Ojo Caliente. Ojo Caliente is the westernmost of the farming villages, its source of life the warm springs that bubble out from under the old lava sheet and eventually swell the waters of the Zuni river. Near this village are the ruins of the ancient Zuni pueblo of Hawikuh, also a spring-centered town.

In addition to the Black Rock Dam mentioned above, the government installed five dams at Nutria in 1932-38 and another at Pescado in 1931. The total irrigation system thus formed has a combined capacity of 9,182 acre feet of water, which serves 6,300 acres of both cultivated and pasture land.

The cover on the reservation ranges from the large tracts of ponderosa pine on the plateau (which provide annually 9,036 acres of commercial timber), to the scrub oak, juniper, and piñon found on the lower slopes, and includes sage brush, yucca, and the grasses found in the valley. There is also a light infestation of noxious weeds on the reservation: whorled milkweed, pea vine, and Canadian thistle are the most serious of these.

The Climate

The annual precipitation is approximately the same as that for the Hopi reservation--thirteen inches--most of which falls in the summer season. The presence of permanent streams and numerous large springs draining from the

Continental Divide accounts for the less arid conditions prevailing on the Zuni reservation. However, the heavy summer rains, combined with the lack of sufficient cover, result in considerable erosion of the land. The severe winds of early spring add to the erosion hazard wherever the land cover is sparse. In places, main water channels have cut to depths of thirty-five feet. The soils of the reservation, grading from sandy to sandy-loam, are derived principally from sandstone. There are also limited areas of adobe clay in the valley bottoms.

There is a tremendous daily swing in the temperature of this high, semiarid region. The average maximum daytime temperature during the winter months is 60°, while at night the average minimum is 7° below zero. Similarly, the average maximum temperature during a summer day is 93°, while it drops to 45° in the evening.

Population

What of the number of people who live on this land now, and have lived there in the recent past? In 1910, the Zuni population was 1,664 (Eggan 1950: 176). By 1942 it had grown to 2,319 individuals--1,267 males and 1,052 females. During that span of thirty-two years, there was a slow growth averaging twenty-one individuals per year, or approximately a rate of growth of 1 per cent per annum. This rate of increase was comparable to the overall population increase of the Indians of the United States during the same period, 1.1 per cent (Kluckhohn and Leighton 1946: 17). After World War II, there was a remarkable upswing in population, starting in 1946 with an increase of 368 Zunis in a four-year period, representing a net average gain of 92 individuals per year, or 3.4 per cent increase per annum. This rate of increase may be partially attributed to the return of the young veterans from war service. (See chart, page 7.)

Physical Type and Dress

As to the people themselves, the Zuni adults are short of stature and light of bone. The men are inclined to leanness, while by contrast the women, after bearing several children, increase in weight, so that by middle age obesity is pronounced. Generally speaking, the adult males give an impression of being less stocky and having lighter musculature than the Hopi or the men of the Rio Grande pueblos. Adding to this impression, they have thin faces and small features.

Zuni Population Growth, 1932-50

Source: Census records, United Pueblos Agency, Albuquerque, N. M.

No. of people (y-axis): 1950, 2000, 2050, 2100, 2150, 2200, 2250, 2300, 2350, 2400, 2450, 2500, 2550, 2600, 2650, 2700, 2750, 2800, 2850

Year (x-axis): 1932, 1933, 1934, 1935, 1936, 1937, 1938, 1939, 1940, 1941, 1942, 1943, 1944, 1945, 1946, 1947, 1948, 1949, 1950

There is a considerable range in physical type within the pueblo and a great deal of overlap in type from one pueblo group to the next. Most marriages out of the pueblo are the outcome of social contacts made with girls and boys from the other pueblos while attending government boarding schools in Albuquerque, Santa Fe, or elsewhere. There are a few Zuni married to Navaho.

Style of dress, including the Zuni woman's hair style, is more indicative than physical appearance of the home pueblo, for the Zuni traditional costume differs in certain important details from that of other Indians of the Southwest. The older and more conservative women, in contrast to the school girls, may still be seen wearing their black and indigo mantas[3] made from two pieces of heavy woolen cloth. The front and back pieces of the garment are held together by a whipping of red and green yarn. The manta passes over the right shoulder and under the left arm. A bright sateen undergarment shows at the bottom, and long sleeves made of the same material are also exposed. A white apron and a back drapery of figured cloth, called the pittone, hang over the manta. White buckskin moccasins and leg wrappings are also worn on ritual or gala occasions. A brightly-figured shawl over the head completes the dress. This shawl is worn whenever the woman steps outside her house, and it distinguishes the Zuni women from those of other tribes when they come into Gallup for their weekly shopping. A rich array of silver jewelry encrusted with turquoise--pins up the side of the manta, "squash-blossom" necklaces, brooches, earrings, and finger rings--are all worn in addition to this elaborate dress on every festive occasion.

In the traditional woman's style, the hair is parted in front and brushed to either side, where it is cut just below the ear on a horizontal line. The hair on the back of the scalp is gathered into a chongo, a long bun, and held in place by a brightly-colored cotton band.

The men's clothes are much less distinctive. They consist of levis and work shirts, except on ceremonial occasions when the costuming is tremendously elaborate. Up to a few years ago, the work-a-day dress of the men included a very broad-brimmed cowboy hat, which gave the small man a rather grotesque appearance. But in recent years, this hat style has become outmoded. On winter nights the men wear a plain black blanket set off by a headband of brilliant silk.

Language

Linguists classify the Zuni speech as a separate linguistic stock, distinct from that of other pueblos, and call it Zunian. It is very different in phonology and structure from that of the Navaho or other Pueblo Indians. This is still the language of social discourse. In the past, the older people used Spanish as their lingua franca in trading activities, but during the last thirty years, as the schoolchildren have gained facility in English, it has been replacing Spanish as the "contact" language.

Modernization

Instrumental to the increased contacts noted above and to the innovations noted in the beginning of this chapter has been the great facilitation of communication with the outside world. A well-surfaced gravel road leads out from the main pueblo to Ramah on the east. At a point a few miles beyond the Black Rock Reservoir, a fork in the road leads north to Gallup. In 1949-50 the road was surfaced with a hard top, so that in good weather a Zuni can now reach town in an hour's drive.

Whereas in 1920 there was only one automobile in the pueblo (Parsons 1939: 1, 30), by 1955, almost every family head owned one. Wagons are rarely seen in the main village, as contrasted to the situation in 1940, and even men on horseback are mostly limited to the range or the family farm.

There is a telephone line leading down to the pueblo from Black Rock, and a line from Zuni to Ojo Caliente. Phones are situated at the various missions and trading posts, as well as in several of the Indian Service houses. The Governor of the pueblo also has a phone in his home, so that he may be in ready contact with the office of the subagent and communicate with points outside the reservation.

Another change occurred during the mid-thirties when the public water system was modernized. Women need no longer go out to carry water from centrally situated pumps. It flows from a community standpipe directly into their kitchens. In the early 'forties there were still many pumps located outside the houses, and these, like the wells and springs of an even earlier period, were favorite places for the boys and girls to meet. The Rural Electrification Administration brought power to the community in 1950, and now Coleman gas lamps (which replaced kerosene lamps in the mid-30s)are disappearing at Zuni as rapidly as they are in other rural areas in the United States.

Today there is also a good-sized white community at Zuni, composed of teachers and other government workers, missionaries and their staffs, and traders with their families. All told, the government-employed Anglo population of the pueblo numbers about thirty, of which more than twenty live at Black Rock. The presence of a community of whites has, of course, been an important force for change. The traders, for example, originally carried food and clothing primarily for this Anglo clientele, only to find that the white buying habits have been imitated by the indigenous members of the pueblo.

The influx of government employees started at the end of the last century, when the Department of the Interior established an independent Indian agency at Black Rock. In 1935, during the commissionership of John Collier, the six agencies in New Mexico which heretofore had administered various parts of the pueblos were consolidated in one office at Albuquerque. The agency at Black Rock then assumed the status of a subagency, and the current administrative head was given the authority of an Assistant Superintendent (Aberle 1948: 56). In 1941, the administration of the Ramah Navaho was added to the United Pueblos Agency's jurisdiction, and this became an added responsibility of the staff at Black Rock. There the United Pueblos Agency maintains a field staff, under the direction of the subagent, consisting of six professional men who carry on technical work in the areas of soil and moisture conservation, range management, maintenance engineering, agricultural extension, and medicine. Each of these staff members has Indian assistants. About thirty Zuni are carried on the government payroll. The administration of the school is the immediate responsibility of the school principal, who carries on her work from an office located at the day school in the pueblo.

The medical division maintains a hospital at Black Rock, which also serves the Ramah Navaho and other Navaho areas immediately adjacent to the Zuni reservation. A public health nurse, with an office and quarters near the day school, is part of the medical staff. She administers inoculations, calls on the sick in their homes, and refers all serious cases to the doctor at Black Rock. Over a period of twenty years this public health nurse has built up a highly successful well-baby clinic.[4]

After this rather brief general description of Zuni today, and before we look further into the contemporary picture, our understanding will be deeper if we first briefly review the mythological record that is the Zuni's own interpretation of his past, the scientific record uncovered by archaeologists, and the many historical documents left by the Spanish conquistadores, traders, and others.

CHAPTER 2

ZUNI HISTORY

The Mythological Account

For the Zuni, the middle of the world is on the edge of their own village. This Middle Place, known to them as hepatina, is where their ancestors
long ago settled after many years' search. The sacred spot is marked by a
shrine built of a few slabs of rock, under which lies a subterranean chamber.
It is situated only a few hundred yards to the west of the Christian Reformed
Church, south of the road to Ojo Caliente. Each year at this site, the Shalako,
Messengers of the Gods, deposit prayer plumes and run a ritual race close to
the shrine prior to making their nocturnal entry into the village.

The origin legend, or the "first beginning according to words," as Dr.
Ruth Bunzel literally translates the Zuni phrase, commences:

In this world there was no one at all. Always
Sun came up; always he went in. No one in
the morning gave him sacred meal; no one
gave him prayer-sticks; it was very lonely.
He said to his two children, "You will go into
the fourth womb. Your fathers, your mothers,
kyäetowe, chu-etowe, mu-etowe, thle-etowe,
all the society chiefs, society criers, society
war chiefs, you will bring out yonder into the
light of your Sun father."

Laying their lightning arrow across their rainbow,
they drew it. Drawing it and shooting down, they
entered. [5]

In this fourth underworld the Children of the Sun--called War chiefs in
two of the versions of the origin legend (Parsons 1939: 218)--encountered a

creature with a "slimy horn, slimy tail; he was slimy all over, with webbed hands." The monster asked the Children of the Sun from whence they came, and they told him of their mission. Then the Children of the Sun saw the ancestors of the Zuni and obtained permission from their head rain priests to guide them to the upper world, where the Sun dwelt by himself. In turn, Eagle, Chicken Hawk, and other birds, then Locust were sent up, seeking the upper world. Locust got as far as the third world, but his strength failed. He could not make it. Finally Reed Youth was successful and led the people to the upper world, where it was so bright that they were forced to close their eyes.

In this way the ancestors of the Zuni reached the upper world. Then followed a series of adventures in their quest for hepatina, where they founded their village, Itiwani. Nowadays the Zuni themselves, in referring to their village, call it by several terms: Itiwawa or Shiwanakwe, both of which mean "Middle Place," and sometimes Hollonawa, "Ant Place," which more specifically refers to a section of the town on the south bank of the river (Kroeber 1917: 202; Hodge 1910: 1016). They use the term "Ashiwi," "the flesh," in referring to themselves when speaking in their own language, and "Zuni" when speaking in English. [6]

As in the origin legends of people the world over, this legend also deals with the etiology of both natural and supernatural phenomena. For example, the origin of the Mexican people and of witches is described with this ominous and prophetic warning:

We [Mexicans and witches] are to be with you
people because this world is small. As it becomes
crowded, we shall kill some of the people [Parsons
1939: 1, 220]. [7]

In the course of this long period of wandering, animals such as the snake and the turtle are created. The koyemshi, ritual clowns of Zuni, are born of the incestuous union of brother and sister; the first dancing of the kok'okshi, the most sacred of the rain dances, occurs; the first appearance of clans and of corn, and in fact the origin of all that is most precious to the Zuni, is accounted for. This is not one myth, but many. Bunzel writes:

There is no single origin myth, but a long series
of separate myths. Each ceremonial group has a
myth which contains, in addition to a general syn-
opsis of early history, the mythological sanction
for its own organization and rituals. There is not,
however, any collected version which is "the talk"
because no mind in Zuni encompasses all knowledge
[Bunzel 1929-30c: 548].

If you ask a Zuni elder for the ancient history of his tribe, this legend in one of its variant forms will be given, a legend sufficient to the needs of a Zuni, steeped in the religion of his people.

The Archaeological Record

Archaeologists tell of other origins (Woodbury 1956: 560). The Zuni, Hopi, and Acoma peoples, as well as the inhabitants of the pueblos in the Rio Grande watershed to the east, are all descendants of ancient peoples with a very long cultural continuum--one which can be traced back to 200 A.D. and earlier. This evolution of progressively complex lifeways, called by the archaeologists Anasazi (a Navaho word meaning "the ancient ones"), developed on the Colorado plateau, in the region where the state borders of Arizona, New Mexico, Utah, and Colorado intersect.

During the course of this great time span a vigorous way of life developed, which has persisted to the present day despite the vicissitudes of a semi-arid climate and recurrent periods of drought. Pueblo culture has also endured waves of peoples who have moved into the territory--Athabaskan migrants from the north, ancestors of the present-day Apache and Navaho peoples, and, much later, Europeans, first the Spanish, by way of their colonies in the New World, and then, in the nineteenth century, the Anglo-American settlers.

A brief sketch drawn from this tremendously detailed archaeological record--under process of examination for over eighty years--is helpful in appreciating the pueblo tradition of which Zuni is part.

The economic base of this pueblo culture sequence was agriculture, as it remains today. These people developed a series of crops, of which corn was the most important, supplemented by squash, pumpkins, and beans. As agricultural skills improved, including advanced methods of "flood-water" irrigation and collection and storage of crops--first in baskets and then in pottery containers--the people were able to live in increasingly large and compact villages. These were built of dressed rock and mud mortar, with wooden beams providing support for the roof, so well built that three- and four-story structures were constructed, room piled upon room. Up to 1910 or thereabouts, Zuni was such a multistoried pueblo, as Taos is today.

From crude beginnings sometime around 500 A.D., pottery making was developed into a fine art. A great variety of designs, types of clay, and techniques of manufacture developed, but the same basic methods of building up the structure from coils of clay, without the help of a potter's wheel, were used thousands of years ago and continue to be used in twentieth-century Zuni and the other pueblos.

While we have no direct evidence that pueblo religion a thousand years ago was organized around rain-making and fertility cults, the archaeological specimens--feathers, masks, stone fetishes, and a few mural paintings which depict masked figures--all indicate that the focus of religious activity was on the fertility of man, beasts, and crops.

The kiva, the ceremonial "club house" found in all the modern pueblos--round shaped in the eastern villages and square at Hopi and Zuni--provides the archaeologist with the best link between modern and ancient religious life.

Some of these kivas were of tremendous size during the Classic Period (Pueblo III), which lasted from 1050 to about 1300. It was during this time that architecture reached its greatest elaboration, as seen in the ruins at Mesa Verde and Chaco Canyon, 100 to 200 miles northeast of Zuni. The kivas excavated there are round, subterranean structures, with cribbed roofs supported by four wooden or stone pillars. Around the walls are benches, such as those found in the kivas of the present day. Since these structures were built underground, it was essential to provide air for the occupants by means of vents. Near the fireplace, in both the ancient and modern kivas is a small hole in the ground, known to archaeologists by the Hopi word, sipapu, and symbolic of the place of emergence from the underworld.

Sixteen miles northeast of Zuni, in the Nutria area, Dr. Frank Roberts excavated a site known as the "Village of the Great Kivas," where one kiva measured 51 feet in diameter and another measured 75 feet. Details of these structures and associated pottery were much like those in the Chaco Canyon area. At that time, the Zuni area was on the southern edge of a large region of San Juan Anasazi culture, of which Chaco Canyon was a major center. "When most of that area was abandoned in the twelfth and thirteenth centuries the Zuni region remained continuously occupied and probably received some minor population accretions from the deserted area" (Woodbury 1956: 560).

In recent years, Dr. Richard Woodbury has excavated a site which is transitional between the Pueblo III type of ruin at Nutria and the communities of the early historic period first reported by Coronado (Woodbury 1956: 560).

The site uncovered by Woodbury, named Atsinna by his Zuni workmen, was situated on the top of El Morro, where a water supply was assured by natural depressions in the rock and by a pool at the base of the mesa. Here the ancestors of the Zuni had built a village of 500 to 1,000 rooms, forming an approximate rectangle 65 by 100 meters. Spreading out from the base of the mesa were remains indicating that this region had been occupied as early as 700 A.D. and that it was inhabited up to the late fourteenth century, when Atsinna was deserted.

At Atsinna, Woodbury found both a round kiva similar to those found at Nutria (twenty miles to the northwest) and extensively throughout the Pueblo III and earlier horizons in the San Juan river drainage and a rectangular one like that found at Hawikuh by Hodge in the town discovered by the conquistadores in the sixteenth century. This, as noted earlier, is the kiva type of the modern pueblo.

Other ruins inhabited at the same time as Atsinna, and similarly abandoned in the latter part of the fourteenth century, are scattered along the sides of the valley which stretches westward toward Zuni. "It is probable that their occupants moved to the six large villages that make up the early historic Zuni group since these villages had their major growth in the fifteenth to seventeenth centuries" (Woodbury 1956: 561).

Atsinna was not deserted overnight, but over a long course of years, not unlike Oraibi, the Hopi village, where the old part of the pueblo has had a dwindling population for decades. Zuni antecedents thus stretch out through past millennia in all directions--northward to the major focus of Pueblo development, at a later time eastward, where there were contacts with ancestral Acoma, and also to the south. Cremation was reported by Coronado and in excavations at Hawikuh by Hodge, but is no longer practiced at Zuni. This was not a puebloan trait, and may have come in from the Hohokam peoples of southern Arizona.

The social organization of Zuni today is most complex, and, as Woodbury has pointed out, "this complexity derives in part from the disparate antecedents of the Zunis, slowly consolidated over the centuries from formerly independent towns and doubtlessly incorporating from time to time bands of migrants from other areas also" (1956: 562).

The Conquest by Spain

It was during the Pueblo IV era that explorers from Spain came up into the Zuni country, opening the documented period of Zuni history. The first of these explorers to enter the Pueblo country was a Negro named Estevan, from the Barbary Coast. He came as an advance scout for Fray Marcos de Niza, the vice commissary of the Franciscan order in New Spain. Fray Marcos had been commissioned in 1538 by Mendoza, the First Viceroy of New Spain, to seek out "some large and powerful villages, four and five stories high" (Hodge 1937: 5).

En route, Fray Marcos heard of seven cities in a country called Cibola,[8] where, according to wishful reports, the people made vessels and armaments of solid gold. He had been in Peru at the time of Pizarro's conquest and probably expected to find riches like those of the Inca in these Indian villages to the north.

On May 21, one of the Indian guides who had gone in advance with Estevan returned to report the death of Estevan at the hands of the people of Cibola. According to the report, Estevan had sent messengers ahead of him into the village. The messengers had angered the people, who then told them to leave. In spite of this, Estevan was not deterred and immediately proceeded into the town. Again his entrance was refused. He was placed in a large house outside the pueblo. There are conflicting stories in the chronicles as to the cause of his death. One story has it that he was trying to escape; another, that he had assaulted the Zuni women. It is also possible that the Zuni people had drawn lines on the ground and told the soldiers not to cross on pain of death, as they were reported to have done when Coronado and his men approached the village during the ensuing year. This "line of closure" made with sacred meal is a ritual Pueblo method of restricting action (Hodge 1937: 41, as quoted in Parsons 1939: 1, 363). The death of Estevan was a portent of what was to come: two hundred years of conflict with the Spanish invaders.

Within a few days, Fray Marcos approached the village, but did not enter. "But finally I feared, considering the danger, and that if I should die there would be no knowledge of this land, which in my estimation, is the largest and best of all yet discovered" (Hodge 1937: 27).

As a result of Marcos' reports, Viceroy Mendoza sent Coronado and a large body of soldiers to explore the country. Coronado and his men entered the pueblo in 1540, but only after a pitched battle with the Indians. Coronado was wounded, but finally the natives were overcome and abandoned the town. They joined the women and children, who had already left and sought refuge on top of Toyallane. (This often became their refuge during further conflict with the Spaniards.) Coronado's hungry army feasted on the corn and other foods that they found stored in the pueblo and, after a time, passed on to the Rio Grande.

Hawikuh was the pueblo where this battle took place and where Estevan had been killed the year before. It was the southernmost settlement of the Zuni people, and hence the first to be reached by a party coming from the south. The pueblo is described as follows in one of the chronicles:

> everything is the reverse of what he [de Niza]
> said, except the name of the city and the large
> stone houses. For, although they are not deco-
> rated with turquoises, nor made of lime nor of
> good bricks, nevertheless they are very good
> houses, with three and four and five stories,
> where there are very good apartments and good
> rooms with corridors, and some very good rooms
> under ground and paved, which are made for

winter, and are something like a sort of hot
baths [a letter from Coronado to Mendoza,
quoted in Hodge 1937: 49].

The latter reference is to the kivas, where the men gathered in the winter.
Because of the heat in these underground structures, the Spaniards called them
estufas, or stoves, which became the Spanish term for kiva.

Castañeda, a foot soldier and chronicler of the expedition, noted that
the Cibola people "have priests whom they call papas. These are the elders."
This, as Hodge points out, is the only Zuni word, except for place names,
that appears in any of the chronicles of the expedition. It is readily identified, as it is still used as the word for "elder brother" and is employed to
designate ceremonial as well as kin relationship.

There were five other villages in addition to Hawikuh, making six in
all. "The seven cities" simply conformed to European number ritual, which
favors seven (just as the Zuni and other American Indians favor four). The
complete list of these six villages is first mentioned in the account of the
Rodriquez-Chamuscado expedition, which visited Zuni in 1581, approaching,
this time, from the east. The first town encountered was K'iakima, situated
at the southwestern base of Toyallane, reported to have some 75 houses of two
and three stories. Next they saw Matsaki, located at the northwestern base
of the same mesa, which had 100 houses, four- and five-stories high, arranged
in compounds. Following down the valley, Halona(wa), adjacent to the site
of the modern pueblo, was reached, and reported as having 45 houses; then
Kwakina, which had been reoccupied after Coronado passed, four miles down
the river, with 60 houses; and finally Hawikuh and, on the mesa nearby,
Kechipawan (Hodge 1937: 61). An estimate places the total population of
these villages in the sixteenth century between 3,000 and 3,500 (Hodge 1937:
117).

The influence of the Europeans was relatively slight during the sixteenth
century as compared to the century that followed. The center of colonization
in the sixteenth century was further east in the Rio Grande valley, and contacts
were therefore limited to the entradas, or expeditions, mentioned above, which
of course introduced some trade goods and left behind a few stragglers of
"Christian Indians" from Mexico. The Spaniards took little interest in the Zuni
and their lands, since they had neither gold nor silver, and since the well-
watered Rio Grande area to the east provided better farmlands for the colonizers.

Early Missions

In the seventeenth century, however, there was renewed interest in Cibola, this time not for plunder but for souls to be saved. The first mission was established in 1629, ninety years after Hawikuh was first seen by Estevan. There, probably at Hawikuh:

> A house was bought for lodging of the Religious, and at once was the first church of that province, where the next day was celebrated the first Mass. And hoisting the triumphal Standard of the Cross, possession was taken, as well in the name of the Roman See as in that of the Imperial [throne] of Spain [Hodge 1937: 82].

At first, all seemed to go well: "they were knowing people and of good discourse; beginning at once to serve the Religious by bringing them water, wood, and what was necessary" [Hodge 1937: 83].

Fray Roque de Figueredo (who prior to this had preached in the Aztec tongue), Fray Francisco de la Madre de Dios, a lay brother, and three soldiers formed this Franciscan Mission group. Although several of the caciques (Zuni priests) and some others submitted to baptism, there was evidently a growing resentment against the interlopers. Three years later a new member of the mission group, Fray Francisco Letrado, who appears to have been of a most zealous nature, was killed upon chiding some idolators who delayed in attending Mass. The Zuni shot him down with arrows, carried off the corpse, scalped it, and thereupon held a scalp dance (Hodge 1937: 91 ff.). Five days later another friar was similarly murdered. The Zuni then fled to Toyallane, their place of refuge, where they remained for three years.

About 1643, eight years after the Zuni returned to live in the pueblos in the valley, the mission at Hawikuh was re-established, and another mission was established at Halona. The priest who lived at Halona also served churches in the other pueblos, including the church at Hawikuh. In 1670, the Hawikuh missionary, Fray Pedro de Avila y Ayala, was murdered by the Apache. His remains were recovered and interred at Halona by the resident priest, Fray Juan Galdo. The Apache also burned the mission to the ground, and from that time on it was abandoned (Hodge 1937: 201).[9] But the villagers remained, even in the face of repeated Apache raids.

In 1680, the Zuni joined the Pueblo Revolt, led by Popé, an Indian of San Juan. The Pueblo Indians were determined to drive their Spanish oppressors out of the country. Over four hundred Spaniards were killed, including the Franciscan missionaries, one of whom was Fray Juan Galdo at Halona. In fear of reprisals, the Zuni retreated once more to their refuge on the mesa top and were still living there in 1692, when Diego de Vargas visited the area on his campaign of reconquest. On this occasion, three hundred children were baptized. De Vargas proceeded on to the Hopi country, leaving behind a garrison of twenty-five soldiers among the Zuni.

The Zuni came down from the mesa and built the village that we know as Zuni today, on the river bank across from where Halona once stood. The population of this village was derived from Hawikuh and Halona, which at the time of the Pueblo Revolt had become the main pueblos, and which in turn had derived populations from the six villages inhabited in the sixteenth century.

In 1699, a new mission was established, dedicated to Our Lady of Guadalupe (Parsons 1939: 2, 874). Though this mission stands in ruins today, the Zuni continue to bury their dead in the attached cemetery. Now located in the center of Zuni, it originally stood to the east of the pueblo, which has since grown around it (Kroeber 1917: 200).

Conflict with the Spanish peoples was not at an end. This time the soldiers caused trouble, treating the Indians harshly and ordering them about: "and furthermore most of them lived in concubinage, some even with married Indian women" (Robinson 1944: 110). On the morning of March 4, 1703, just after Mass had been said, three Spaniards who had been living in the pueblo in exile from Santa Fe were murdered. This time the priest was not touched. Most of the Indians sought refuge on the top of Toyallane, while others fled to Sichomovi, a Hopi village. There is evidence in the chronicles that the Zuni who took part in this last outbreak were under the influence of the Hopi, who had only a short time before destroyed the pueblo of Awatovi, where a mission had been established. The governor in Santa Fe, Pedro Rodriguez Cubero, now sent troops out to Halona to rescue the friar, whose petitions to remove the offending soldiers and exiles he had ignored previous to the uprising. The padre returned to Zuni in 1705 and induced the Indians to come down from the mesa. Evidently the mission built up its following once more, for in 1744 two priests were assigned to Halona (Robinson 1944: 110).

During this first decade of the eighteenth century the Hopi raided the Zuni villages, where most of the Indians had by now embraced the Catholic faith The Zuni, in their turn, raided Hopi villages. This strife between the two groups continued until the Hopi made peace with the Zuni (even though they refused to do so with the Spaniards).

Later Missions

In the opening two decades of the nineteenth century, the Navaho and Apache were menacing the pueblos on all sides of their range, as well as the Spanish colonists in the Rio Grande valley. The raids reached such proportions that it was no longer safe to attempt to carry on mission activities, and in 1821 the Franciscans withdrew from Zuni. It was not until a hundred years later that the mission was re-established.

During this hundred-year interlude, the Catholic Church was not completely out of touch with the pueblo. For example, in 1863 Bishop Lamy came to Zuni (Fuller 1943: 52), and from time to time during the early twentieth century it was visited by priests from Gallup.

Near the close of this hundred-year period (about 1900), during which the Catholic Church was less active and had withdrawn its mission from Zuni, a Protestant sect, the Dutch Reformed Church (now called the Christian Reformed Church), established a mission and school on the south bank of the river.[10] During the ensuing years, this Church has built up a steady school attendance, with 139 students enrolled in 1942-43, but Church attendance is still small. The three or four families that are regular in attendance have taken over the faith. The question of how many converts there are who have given up Zuni religious practices in favor of Christianity remains open for further investigation.

Changes Wrought

The Spanish and Christian Church history of Zuni represents the best-documented part of Zuni history, with the exception of the anthropological work done in the recent past. We can summarize some of the above material in terms of the principal critical changes brought about during the Spanish period.

First a word of caution, however, for, as Parsons has pointed out in numerous papers dealing with Pueblo religion and social organization, the Pueblos were acculturated to Hispanic culture over a much longer period than they have been to North European culture. Here, as in all Latin American countries, to separate the Spanish traditions from the aboriginal Indian customs requires close analysis and is frequently an impossible task. Only a few of the more obvious borrowed elements can be mentioned here, previous to a more complete presentation of Zuni religion in a later chapter.

Zuni religion has borrowed heavily from the Spanish, especially in regard to death and burial practices. The washing of the body, the all-night vigil, and the wailing of the women attest to Spanish origin (Parsons 1916a). The observation of All Souls' Day, when the Zuni children go from house to house singing a Latin-derived song, and the parading of the Santo during the harvest dance in the fall of the year are evidence of the tremendous influence of the Catholic Church. Spanish witchcraft beliefs probably diffused in great measure during the period of occupancy and fused with the aboriginal sorcery patterns (Parsons 1927).[11]

In her earlier work, Parsons attributed great importance to the influence of the Christian Church on the Katchina cult (the masked dancers) and played up the parallels between Christian Saints and their Pueblo equivalents.[12] However, the Katchina cult, which had Zuni as its source or origin, may be interpreted as a nativistic movement, i.e. a negative reaction to an enforced Christianity which had as its goal the suppression of native religion. The end effect was that the Katchina cult seems at first glance to dominate Zuni religious life, whereas, in fact, it simply obscures from notice the other more central religious practices concerned with war and curing.

In addition to their influence on the religious life of the people, the Franciscan priests certainly had an effect in changing the economic life as well. During their time, wheat, oats, and other grains were introduced. In fact, the cultivation of grain, other than corn, accounted for the growth in population of the farming villages, where water was more plentiful for irrigation than in the Zuni valley proper.

Along with grain, the Zuni adopted the threshing floor, a circular flagstone area where the grain is spread out and horses are driven around to separate the grain from the stalks. Despite the more recent introduction of mechanical threshing equipment, many Zuni cling to the older method. Cattle and horses were also introduced by the Spanish conquerors. The Missions maintained their own herds. Capture of this livestock was one of the objects of the Apache raids, and large herds were driven off when the Apache destroyed Hawikuh in 1672 (Hodge 1937: 98). Other farm animals, such as pigs and chickens, were also taken over but in more restricted numbers.

The introduction of peach trees was still another important influence on the eating habits of the people. Today peach orchards are largely confined to the lands at the bottom of the mesas to the north and south of the village. There they benefit by protection from the wind, run-off water from the mesas, and the reflected heat from the rocks.

The chili pepper, too, was brought in by the Spaniards from farther south. Ever since the late nineteenth century and probably dating back several hundred years before that, the growing of chili and onions has been women's work, in contrast to the cultivation of corn, beans, squash, and grains, which is men's work. The women plant their gardens along the river bank in small hand-irrigated plots, ridged with high earthen borders to form a grid. They have been called "waffle gardens" in the popular literature. (See Plate No. 2, Aerial View of Zuni, 1947.)

It is highly probable that the civil government of the pueblo also dates from the Spanish period. In aboriginal times the leadership of the pueblo was in the hands of a high council of priests. The Spaniards had difficulty dealing with them, because of religious secrecy, and encouraged the establishment of a secular governorship, it being the governor's duty to deal as a middle man between the caciques and the outside authorities.

Relations with the United States Government

The many secular services rendered by the Catholic Church during the Spanish period became the function of the Indian Service and the Protestant Missions during the last century. A subagency was established at Black Rock, and farm, health, and educational activities became a primary concern, as well as the maintenance of the enlarged irrigation system and the public water supply in the village. Along with these services, including the free schooling made available by the government and by the two missions,[13] there was on the part of some Zuni an increased feeling of dependence on the government, a trend the present United Pueblo Service is trying to counteract, as is shown in greater detail in a later chapter.

In order to bring this brief historical sketch up to date, we might also note that during the past century relations with the outside world were considerably improved. The original Spanish land grant was greatly enlarged when the reservation was established in 1877. As noted in Chapter 1, additional lands have been added to the reservation since that date. This is an Executive Order reservation, not a treaty reservation. There has never been any open conflict between the Zuni and the United States government such as existed during the nineteenth century between the government and the Navaho (Fuller 1943: 74 ff.)[14] Neither has there been bitter strife over the encroachment of the Navaho, as was the case with the Hopi. Nor do we find the difficulty that has come about as a result of settlement on checkerboard lands, such as exists at the present time among the Ramah Navaho.

Other events, like the stock reduction program and the all-important history of the traders and their relationship to Zuni life, will be dealt with in the next chapter, where we concern ourselves with a more detailed picture of Zuni economic life.

CHAPTER 3

FARMERS, HERDERS, AND SILVERSMITHS

The Zuni, like the other Pueblo peoples, were farmers centuries before the coming of the Spaniards. Their religion, which was integral to their
agricultural arts, stressed fertility worship and weather control. In Zuni rationale, corn and other crops are grown first by attention to religious duty,
and second by tilling the soil.[15]

Early Innovations

With the coming of the Spaniards, new crops and domesticated animals were introduced, as was mentioned in Chapter 2, and new implements
were added to Zuni technology. The most important of the new plants was
wheat, and of the European farm animals, the horse, the ox, and the burro
became valuable in facilitating transportation as well as farm work. The
horse was used for long journeys and not for work in the fields, the latter being
a job for the ox, which pulled the plow and the carreta, a two-wheeled cart.
Oxen were used in this way until the late nineteenth century, when Cushing
reported on agricultural practices. The burro, in Cushing's day and earlier,
was used primarily for hauling wood and water into the village. Sheep and
cattle were also introduced and were to become most important in latter-day
Zuni economics.

Another important factor was the introduction of firearms. These
weapons and the horse were also obtained by the Navaho and Apache, and
made more effective their aggressive warfare on the settled Pueblo peoples during the eighteenth and nineteenth centuries. For the Zuni, the gun became
primarily a defensive weapon in holding off the Athabaskan raiders, and an
improvement upon the bow and arrow in the hunt.[16]

These innovations broadened the economic base. With the coming of the horse, trading activities were intensified with the other Pueblos to the east and with the Hopi to the north. The ox-drawn carreta enabled them to carry produce in greater quantities from the fields to the pueblo. The diet became more diversified with the addition of wheat, mutton, and beef, a change from the aboriginal diet of venison and antelope. Handwoven woolen textiles were added to the aboriginal cotton fabrics and rabbit-skin blankets, thus providing warm and less bulky garments for winter wear.

These and other changes came about during the Spanish period and had been well integrated with the aboriginal way of life when the first descriptive reports were made by Cushing, Bourke, Stevenson, and others, starting in 1879. However, even at that time Zuni was far on the western frontier, three or four days by horse from the Rio Grande towns. Except for the trading of excess agricultural products with other Pueblo peoples (and the Navaho during periods of truce) and with the Spanish-Americans, Zuni was economically self contained. Cushing's article in the Century Magazine exploited this very fact (Cushing 1882-83). Here was the American Indian living his untouched "pagan" existence, a way of life that had long ago ceased to exist among the Indians of the eastern seaboard.

Trading Posts

This economic independence diminished after the railroad was extended to Gallup in the 1880s. The railroad enabled the mercantile companies in the Rio Grande valley to distribute goods to individual traders. The first trader at Zuni was Douglas Graham, who was running a small store there in 1879 (Cushing 1882-83: 26, 35). Within the same decade, the first trading post was established on the Navaho reservation at Ganado, some eighty miles to the north of Zuni.

The Zuni trade depended on their agricultural surplus, primarily wheat, some corn, and livestock. In exchange for these, the Zuni purchased matches, iron cooking utensils, yard goods, and luxury goods such as coffee, tobacco, and sweets. During the last two decades of the nineteenth century, such a trade could support one Anglo trader and several Zuni traders. Probably because of the growing importance of the sheep economy, the trading business became more and more dependent on outside capitalization, and the small Indian trader lost what in effect had been a grocery store business to the commercial traders who were backed by the large mercantile companies and wholesale traders in Gallup.[17] The first two decades of the twentieth century saw the founding of three trading companies: Vanderwagen Brothers, Charles Kelsey, and C. G. Wallace. The presence of four trading posts, three of which are very prosperous, speaks for the change in Zuni economy.

The forty years between Cushing's residence at Zuni in the 1880s and the years following World War I saw Zuni change from a relatively self-sufficient village to one dependent in large degree on the outside market, both for consumer goods and for sale of farm and range products. Both the Zuni trader and the Indian Service were responsible for the economic development of the reservation. The former was primarily interested in selling the Zuni a great variety of store goods, while the latter was concerned with education, health, resources, and the improvement of technical facilities. In order to build up the purchasing power of his customers, the trader encouraged the Zuni to increase their herds and to improve the quality of their livestock. In contrast to the concern of the Indian Service, the trader was less interested in agricultural produce, which was never very important as a trade item.[18] Ultimately, here, as elsewhere in the Southwest, there was a depletion of the basic resources. The large herds encouraged by the trader overgrazed the land, and the resulting soil erosion led the government to enforce a stock reduction program in 1942. This action brought about friction between the government and the traders, as well as between the government and the Indians. Stock reduction was as hard on the pocketbook of the trader as it was on that of the Indian.

The Growth of Silvercraft

The traders had thus built up Indian markets for the mercantile companies. Goods manufactured in the East, goods processed in the Middle West, and a thousand and one household items from all over the United States found a community with an expanding economy and a desire for manufactured goods. In order to increase further the purchasing power of the Zuni and also to provide themselves with another product which could be sold on the outside market, the traders developed the output of the Zuni silversmiths as a commercial item. In the 1880s, this handcraft specialization was comprised of a few smiths who had learned their skills from the Navaho. Their wares were traded with others in the pueblo and with other Pueblo Indians. Economically, this craft was of little importance. But with the coming of the railroad, tourists traveling through the Southwest on their way to or from California bought Indian jewelry on the train and station platform. The hawking of "curios" (especially Indian-fashioned silver jewelry) on train platforms and in the coaches was introduced by the Fred Harvey Company, and was the beginning of what has developed into a major business in the Southwest. The curio trade depended in the beginning on Navaho craftsmen, who exchanged their rugs and jewelry for store goods. Later, after the first World War, the trade spread to Zuni, where the enterprising storekeepers stimulated interest in a distinctive type of jewelry which depends upon many small sets of turquoise or inlay work of shell and stone for its decorative effect (Adair 1944).

Between 1925 and 1945, jewelry and curio handcraft developed into a major source of Zuni revenue, estimated as high as 65 per cent of the total cash income of the pueblo by the end of the 1940s. In addition to jewelry, the women and girls made beaded novelties for the traders. Development of a cash economy brought about a great many changes in the culture of the people, which will be analyzed more fully in a later chapter.

Irrigation

During the territorial period, all Pueblo Indians were administered from Santa Fe. It was not until the close of the century that an agency was opened at Black Rock. Prior to that, Graham, the first trader, had also served as government farmer. During the first thirty years of the present century, the Indian Service developed the water resources on the reservation. The Black Rock dam was constructed over a three-year period from 1904 to 1907.[19] The immediate effect of this project was to draw back to the village many residents of the farming villages. A farmer of Ojo Caliente (and one of the best of the older Zuni farmers) reported:

> Then the people in Caliente began to hear about
> using water for irrigating at Zuni. Some were anxi-
> ous to go back to Zuni and take up old land and stay
> at Zuni and save trouble of moving out every year.
> If [it is] bad weather you sometimes had to stay over-
> night. In those days it was much worse. By saving
> all that trouble of going to Zuni for sacred dances,
> by having water there, half of the town remained at
> Zuni, half here. Today there is only forty families
> in Caliente [Mills 1947].

Ever since prehistoric times, the Zuni have made use of the natural springs on their lands and have built small irrigation systems wherever such springs or streams provided water. In 1881, Captain John Bourke reported: "This Nutria valley contains I should say about 4,000 A. [acres] of arable land, 400 A. [acres] being irrigated by ditches laid out with wonderful skill" (Bloom 1936: 111). The development of improved irrigation facilities in the farming villages was undertaken at a later date. It is reported by one of the residents of Ojo Caliente that this work was accomplished by the Zuni themselves, without government assistance. During the late twenties (or possibly the early thirties) the farmers of that community built a reservoir for impounding the waters flowing from the large spring nearby. During the Collier administration, federal aid was given for the enlargement of this reservoir, and

in the forties additional dams were constructed at Nutria and Pescado. Also
during the Collier administration, wells were drilled and stock tanks were constructed on the sheep and cattle ranges.

The Zuni do not use water as efficiently as the Hopi, who have much
less of it, nor are they as systematic in its usage as are the Rio Grande pueblos.
At the present time, and possibly extending back far into the past, there is
in Zuni no formal native control or supervision of water distribution. The
governor calls the men out to clean the ditches in the spring, and the
tenientes do the same in the farming villages. There is often considerable
delay before the job is done. One of the Indian field staff reports:

> They don't have any method of irrigating. It
> looks as if they do it any old way. There is no
> scheme for one person having the water at a set
> time. As a result they all open their laterals at
> the same time and get just a thin stream of water.
> They just argue about it. Time after time I've
> taken this up in meetings, but I haven't gotten
> anywhere.

Cleaning of the ditches and control of water usage by enforced rotation is
better handled in certain of the Rio Grande pueblos, where there is a whole
group of elected officers known as mayordomos, whose duty it is to supervise
irrigation (Aberle 1948: 43).[20]

Farm Extension

Steady progress in scientific agriculture has been made during the last
twenty-five years under the direction of the present farm extension agent. He
has had an up-hill fight all the way. It has been mentioned that many aspects
of agriculture are closely tied to religion, and therefore ritualized, especially
the growing of the original crops: corn, pumpkins, squash, and beans. The
religious Zuni is loath to change his methods of growing these crops. The
farm agent has made a contribution by getting the school children interested
in 4-H Club work and in initiating, along with the school staff, fruit and vegetable canning and preserving. During World War II, several Zuni men from
the Nutria area became interested in truck gardening on a commercial scale,
but this did not take hold in the main village, where the women still grow the
garden crops in their small hand-watered plots.

Resistance to new agricultural methods continues. Only a few Zuni
make use of the valuable animal manure available, even after years of coach-
ing by the farm agent and others. On several occasions, manure has been sold
to outside dealers. The Zuni also resist the planting of trees. They believe

that if a tree is planted and takes root, it "shortens your life." One of the
successful farmers at Caliente, who has been an innovator for many years,
planted a row of cottonwood trees as a windbreak, only to have them all cut
down by his neighbors. This was many years ago, but trees are still not
planted, with the exception of the fruit trees in the orchards along the mesas.
Insofar as these were introduced by Europeans, their cultivation is not so surrounded by religious strictures. During the postwar period, Zuni farmers
turned down the land leveling program offered to them by the Agricultural
Adjustment Administration. The reason for this is not known to the authors.
It may be surmised that the Zuni were afraid that if they had their lands
leveled free of charge, except for their own labor involved, it might entail
obligations which they would have to pay back to the government. This has
been the attitude of the Zuni and other Indian groups of the southwest on
several occasions when federal aid has been offered.

The Zuni may also have had religious sanctions against land leveling,
just as they have had in some of the pueblos in times past against the use of
the plow. Such modern agricultural implements destroy the fertility of the
land when long cuts are made in it, they believe. There should only be spo-
radic openings, such as were made with the traditional digging stick, which
was used to impregnate the earth with seed.[21]

Available statistics, based upon annual crop reports, indicate that the
total worth of crops in 1950 was more than five times their value in 1930.
The statistics read as follows:

1930	$12,330
1935	37,888
1940	55,483
1945	45,787
1950	68,655

[United Pueblos Agency, Annual Extension Reports.]

A breakdown of three major crops during the period 1940-47 reveals that there
was an over-all increase in these crops up to 1943, and that production then
dropped, with over 200 men serving in the armed forces and additional men
and women engaged in war work. This situation was prolonged during the
years immediately after the war, for in 1945 and 1946 silver work was bringing
high prices, and many men bent their energies in that direction. Furthermore,
many of the veterans and their families lived on Veteran's Administration self-
employment or educational benefits. All of this tended to discourage the
planting of crops until 1947, when cash payments began to fall off (see Table I).

Table I

Number of Acres Harvested per Crop

Year	Corn	Wheat	Beans	Melons
1940	650	1,276	230	105
1941	780	1,502	230	100
1942	1,172	1,366	237	79
1943	1,200	1,180	276	81
1944	1,160	845	258	95
1945	1,111	451	76	---
1946	926	393	154	57
1947	934	408	277	121

[United Pueblos Agency, Annual Extension Reports.]

In 1948, several Zuni, with the encouragement of the subagent, organized a group of veterans to study farming. They obtained a young instructor trained at the agricultural college at Las Cruces, and twenty men enrolled in the course. The assessed outcome of this training is not available at this writing. Possibly these younger men will break down some of the old resistance, since they shared a certain set of common experiences away from the pueblo and may be willing to face as a group the criticism usually directed at the isolated individual who adopts new practices. In agriculture, as in other phases of pueblo life, we find a sensitivity to ridicule which runs through the culture and acts as a block to innovations of all sorts. The innovator is criticized for "trying to act like a white man," and the slightest changes are singled out for notice. If the individual following the instruction of his teacher puts manure on his crops and fails to bring in a good crop he is teased severely. This of course discourages not only the particular individual but all others who abandon or who think of abandoning the old ways.

It is quite possible that these younger farmers will break away from the habits of the older farmers. In the future they may learn to fertilize their fields, rotate crops more systematically, and get up early in the morning to work their fields--practices that the farm agent has introduced to a limited number of farmers. Such changes in traditional habits will come only with a motivation quite different from that of the elder man, who relies to a great extent upon the supernatural. He spends long hours away from his fields in order to make the crops grow, which from the point of view of the modern agriculturist is pure neglect.

There will have to be an additional incentive to raise a food "surplus," as subsistence farming has been the goal of these farmers for generations. This may come about through economic motivation, which is already well established in the realm of silvercraft and livestock raising. It may also come about through the increased prestige that is attached to possession of cash and all that it can buy. Certainly the natural resources for greatly increased crop production exist, especially for vegetables and fruit.

Livestock

Stock raising is much more important than agriculture as a cash pursuit. Figures reveal that cattle sales approximately match crop income, while income from sheep products (lambs, wool, and pelts), greatly exceed these two activities combined. In fact, the income from sheep is over five times that of the agricultural produce that reaches the market (see Table II).

Table II

Breakdown of Total Income from Sales of
Agricultural and Livestock Products

Year	Crops	Cattle (beef)	Sheep	Wool	Pelts
1944	4,440	5,330	23,766	50,160	4,650
1947	24,658	22,018	90,346	38,512	4,243
1950	27,604	24,791	79,804	55,020	5,800

[United Pueblos Agency, Annual Extension Reports.]

This is in addition to sheep, which are home consumed. It has been estimated that over 2,000 sheep are slaughtered during the Shalako ceremony and possibly as many as 6,000 in the course of the whole year.

Division of labor and ownership. Traditionally, the women own the crops once they are brought in from the fields. The men have complete control over their cultivation in the fields, including attention to the ritual, without which they will not grow. However, once they have passed over the threshold the crops are taken into the storage room, where they are shared by a group of sisters of a matrilineally-reckoned family line.

The men divide their time as farmers between working on the fields of their wives, i. e. producing the crops for what may be called the family of procreation to which their children belong, and caring for the crops of the natal family, i. e. the fields belonging to their mother's line. To each family they owe economic responsibility and to these two lines of descent there is a patterned system of mutual obligation which runs through the social life of the group. However, first priority goes to the support of one's wife and children.

Although the harvested crops belong to the women, the land on which they are grown is not thought of as being essentially women's property, and the land may be passed down through both the female and male lines. The foregoing is of long standing and does not represent a very recent change (Cushing 1920: 125 ff.). Women do not have the same control over wealth derived from the herds of sheep and cattle. Traditionally this is men's property, and they may have more of a free hand in the distribution and use of the cash derived from the sale of the livestock. Bunzel has pointed out that the rising importance of the trading post transactions based on cattle and sheep sales have given the men an independence of the women that they did not once enjoy (Bunzel 1940). The sheep are individually owned by men, and each is ear-marked according to its owner. A group of related males herd their sheep together, and a distinctive brand is stamped on the back of each animal with red paint. These brands are registered at Black Rock and preclude possible arguments over ownership. The cooperating group, which shares in the sale of both the lamb crop and the wool clip, cuts across the household groupings into which the men are married, i. e. the family of procreation, and tends to follow clan lines.

This is an oversimplification of the actual situation, for we find that today sheep are not only owned by men but also by some women who have inherited sheep from their fathers. In this case the sheep are cared for by the woman's husband, who takes his turn herding along with his brothers-in-law (his wife's brothers).

Sheep management. The group of related males has a sheep camp located on part of the range which has become theirs by virtue of use rights. Each man in such a group herds the flock for a period of about two weeks. At many sheep camps, there are permanently built houses to which the men move in the spring during lambing and shearing season. One or two of the women accompany them out to the camp and cook meals during this period of intensive work. Temporary camp sites are established on the range, where the herder pitches his tent. These sites are shifted from time to time, so that the whole of the area is grazed during the course of the year. Each day the sheep are watered at tanks supplied by windmill pumps (installed by the government during the 1930s), and then herded back to the temporary camp, where they are put in a brush corral for the night.

The brothers and other male relatives of the herder come out to camp several times a week to bring food for the next period. Many of the Zuni find herding a distasteful task and often hire younger men to take their turns. Payment is in cash. The going wage in 1947 was two dollars a day, or it could be paid in ewes; if the herder is retained over a long period of time he may secure a share in the lamb crop. By herding for others, many a Zuni has built up his own flock over a period of years. Retaining such herders is nothing new, nor are the herders always Zuni. Some families hire Navaho herders, or Spanish-American families who establish themselves out at the "ranch" houses for many months at a time. Thus the wealthy Zuni is able to attend to other matters in the village and still superintend his sheep interests by short visits to the camp.

Stock reduction. As was mentioned earlier, a stock reduction program was inaugurated on the Zuni reservation in 1942. The goal of this federal program was to reduce soil erosion by cutting down the size of the flocks and herds to the carrying capacity of the range. At that time there were 25,808 sheep, 788 cattle, and 798 horses on the reservation. Over a period of five years, the number of sheep was reduced to 18,665, while the number of cattle was held about the same (813), and the number of horses increased to 1,192. This was close to the carrying capacity of the reservation. Prior to stock reduction, starting in the midthirties, the United Pueblos Agency initiated a stock improvement program. In the decade following 1938, a total of 60 purebred Hereford bulls and 952 rams of an improved type were purchased by the Zuni. Over the short period of five years, as a result of the sheep improvement, the wool clip increased from 121,096 pounds in 1938 to 160,200 pounds in 1943. This was the largest wool output of any of the groups under the administration of the United Pueblos Agency, exceeding even the production of Laguna, the next largest producer, by some 40,000 pounds (Aberle 1948: 86ff.).

While this reduction did tend to cut down on the big herds, which during the early years of the century sometimes numbered as many as 5,000 sheep,[22] there is by no means an equal distribution of sheep wealth today. Ther are at least four flocks of 1,000 sheep or more, and approximately a fifth of all the Zuni sheep are owned by seven extended families. This of course is not individual wealth, but the sheep and the wealth derived therefrom are shared by groups of males, one of whom in any such group is the largest owner and recognized leader. Like sheep, cattle are also owned by the men, and ownership is concentrated in a few family lines. The herds are grazed on the northern and southern range areas, the former serving as the winter range. All cattle and sheep are sold at an annual sale in the fall, when buyers come in from the outside to bid for the livestock. As can be seen from Table II, cattle are not as important as sheep to Zuni economy.

Tribal Income

As to an over-all picture of Zuni income, the most complete figure available dates from 1942 (United Pueblos Agency 1946). In that year, the total income of the Zuni tribe was computed as being $316,089.55. This amounted to a family income (using 5 as the average family size) of $681.50. The distribution of this income shows that 110 families had an income of from $1,500 to $1,999, and 110 families had an income of $2,000 or over. How much over $2,000 is not stated, and is evidently not known to the Agency (United Pueblos Agency 1946).[23]

The income of the Zuni tribe was probably considerably greater than the official figures show, due to underestimation of the volume of the silver handicraft business carried on by the traders. During the years 1945-46, the peak period in the Zuni curio business, it was estimated by the subagent that the traders' gross volume in this trade amounted to more than $1,500,000. Of this, approximately $900,000 represents pay to the silversmiths, in either cash or store credit, and $600,000 the cost of the silver and turquoise fabricated into jewelry. This sum represents the volume of the business of the four traders in Zuni, and does not take into account the income from jewelry made for the Gallup dealers, which might be estimated at 25 per cent of the reservation sales. During this period, many families made a weekly trip to town in their automobiles to deliver the finished turquoise jewelry and inlay work and to get new orders and materials for the next week.

This cottage industry was so profitable that the number of silversmiths and inlay workers reached a total of 428 (237 men and 191 women) by 1947. The Zuni census of that year reveals a total population of 2,205 residents [24] (see graph of Zuni population growth, Chapter 1, p. 7). Out of approximately 1,674 males and females over fourteen years of age (younger boys or girls rarely practice the craft), one out of three persons spent some of his time at this craft work.[25] This is not to say that all of this number might be called "professional" craftsmen in the sense that this was their sole means of earning a livelihood. Most of them spent only a fraction of their time at the silversmith's bench. However, it can be said that every household had at least one full-time smith, if not several. In addition, a spouse and several of the older children usually assisted the "master craftsman" as they found time.

When the earnings of individuals and families are examined, one can well believe that the craft brought in the total income that is attributed to it.

One man and wife reported selling twenty bracelets for a total of $900. This work took them no more than three weeks. Another smith reported that he cleared $400. in a month, without the help of his wife. An inlay worker netted $150. a month from his work even after the peak of the curio boom had passed. One extremely rapid worker claimed that during the war years he was able to sell silver worth $400. in a week.[26] From 1942 to 1947, and possibly even since that time (although the jewelry market has fallen way off), the income from the silver jewelry industry has exceeded the income from both agriculture and livestock.

During the war, in addition to the money earned from this craft work, there was a great deal of cash derived from the dependency allotments and service pay of over 200 pueblo men in the armed services. This pay meant many more thousands of dollars coming into the village each month. The growth of the jewelry craft and the additional influx of cash derived from government checks to servicemen's families provided the basis for a shift to a cash and wage economy. This same dependence on cash and wage work is evident at other pueblos, such as Laguna and Isleta. However, in these pueblos the shift has occurred over many decades, while at Zuni it has taken place in a few years. One of the government employees who had been in the pueblo for a good many years remarked in 1947 that "Zuni has changed more in the last ten years than during the whole preceding twenty-year period." This shift in the economic base has had reverberations in all aspects of Zuni life. Within the scope of this chapter we can point to some of the changes that are more readily classified with the material and economic life of the people. Changes in civil government, social structure, and religious life will be dealt with in later chapters.

The Changing Economy

We have indicated that agricultural production fell off during the war and postwar years, but we must also realize that the drop was considerably greater than is immediately apparent, for these figures represent the inflationary trend of the local market. Many of the men who once planted extensive fields now plant smaller fields, and many of the younger men, who twenty years ago would have spent most of the growing season out in the fields, now spend the greater part of this time at the silversmith's bench. The money received in return for the silver work, as well as that received through the sale of livestock, will buy both material goods and prestige. The improved house with indoor plumbing, the new expensive automobile, the better clothes, and all of the other changes in the material culture of the Zuni give evidence of this shift in their economic life and in their values as well.

One of the places where this flood of money finds an outlet is in the grocery stores. A self-service grocery opened by one of the oldest trading companies became an immediate success and captured some of the trade that had been going to the Gallup merchants, whose grocery stores attracted Zuni in great numbers every Saturday. The changing food habits of the Zuni are reflected in these purchases. Fresh vegetables have become part of the diet of many families, whereas twenty-five years ago, according to the farm agent, "you couldn't get a Zuni to eat lettuce, cabbage, celery and many of the things they eat now." [27] It is of interest that the Zuni will purchase vegetables from the store even though the country is suited to truck gardens and a large cash return is assured for such produce. In all probability, the men will not grow truck crops to any significant degree because this is traditionally women's work. [28] The Zuni is a conservative farmer, and the older farmers are loath to change habits which are reinforced by religious sanctions and public sentiment. Thus in nutrition programs at Zuni, as in other pueblos, it is easier to get the people to buy fresh vegetables in the store than it is to get them to raise these foods.

In contrast to the above situation, and to the farm situation described below, the craft of the silversmiths has not conflicted as sharply with the sheep economy. For one thing, as has been pointed out, both occupations are closely allied with the cash and trading-post system. However, the major reason is probably related to the work calendar. The sheep are herded by a rotating workgroup of related males. This means that when any one person is relieved of his herding duties he can return to his craft work and forget about the sheep until it is his turn again to herd the flock. The alternation of activity is interrupted only during shearing and lambing season in the spring and during the annual drive to the tribal corrals for the sale of lambs in the fall.

The same division of labor is not so conveniently worked out by the man who used to be a farmer and has now become a silversmith. The crops demand constant attention during the growing season. Thus, the farmer will not take up the craft as readily as will the man who derives much of his income from sheep or cattle. If he does, he will put in most of his time during the winter season, when there is relatively little to do on the farm. [29]

The growing cash economy has produced new economic specialties. Whereas thirty years ago the Zuni specialists were few in number, and only a handful worked for wages, [30] now we find that a third of the pueblo is working for cash and/or store credit. The jack-of-all-trades who is found in economic life on the subsistence level is gradually giving way to the specialist: the silversmith, the government employee, carpenter, railroad worker, livestock man, etc. This was nicely illustrated by a remark made by one of the residents of the pueblo who was questioned about his opinion of the "On-the-Farm Training Program" inaugurated in 1948 by the Veteran's Administration:

A lot of those veterans that have signed up for the
program are silversmiths, they aren't farmers. They
are just after those government [subsistence] checks.
They won't take up farming. They will go back to
silver work when they have finished the course.

The fundamental change in the Zuni economic system and the changing attitudes of the people with regard to wealth are neatly illustrated by com-
paring the village economy of the present day, presented in this chapter, with
that of the mid-twenties, when Ruth Bunzel made her studies of language and
ceremonialism. She wrote:

The Zuni family with whom I lived would never accept direct remuneration for food. They would sell
almost anything else, but to sell food violated their
deepest sentiments. They were insulted if offered
money for food, but would accept "presents" of
money offered as "remembrances" of a visit (Bunzel
1938: 345-46 n.).

Yet when the present writer lived at Zuni, twenty years later, this same
woman cooked meals for sale to Shalako visitors.

Bunzel wrote (1938: 354): "There is only one recognized 'rich' family at Zuni, and they are half breeds."[31]   However, there is documented evidence that by 1943 there were several families which could be called "rich."
A meeting was called by the Agency that year to discuss federal income tax
regulations.[32] The records reveal that seven men reported an income of over
$1,800 from the sale of their livestock. This figure did not include the wool
sales, which would double these figures.[33] Also, computation of the income
of silversmiths reveals that by 1947 the average income from that source alone
was better than $2,000 per craftsman (see p. 33).

Bunzel did note that the profit motive in livestock production was a
force for change in 1926 (Bunzel 1938: 356). The growth of the cash economy
during the intervening years served to encourage the profit motive in other
phases of the economy. The concept that "time is money" has also taken
hold among the wage workers and silversmiths. Even though they are paid
on a piecework basis, they readily translate work accomplished into time consumed. In 1947 it was general practice for these men to hire others to perform less profitable tasks, such as tilling crops or herding sheep, while they
carried on work that brought in a greater immediate cash return. This is also
in contrast to an earlier day (1917), when the Zuni did not hire each other
(see footnote 30). One Zuni who operated a small store in the village complained that there was no pay for taking part in the Harvest Dance, which
heretofore was considered an honor passed down in only a few family lines.

In the same year (1947) one of the stockmen was observed rushing to get away from the pueblo. He said, "I want to get up to Gallup to catch the plane over to Albuquerque. I've got business to attend to there. I will be back home tonight." To be sure this is an extreme case, but it was the action of one of the most successful of the stockmen, and while many of the villagers will gossip about him and say, "He tries to act like a white man," others may come to follow his ways.

Bunzel also wrote (1938: 352):

The outstanding characteristics of the economic system are the strong development of cooperative attitudes and techniques, the corresponding absence of competition and aggressive behavior in general, the dominant role of women in economic affairs, the fluidity of wealth, which implies the absence of acquisitiveness, and a thoroughly realistic attitude toward property, which is valued for direct use and not as an instrument for power or prestige. Power and authority are vested in the possessors of nonmaterial privileges, rituals, songs, fetishes, and war honours, and these are never used for economic ends. The "poor man" is one without ceremonial connections.

Cooperative attitudes have been modified in the last twenty-five years. This is evident in the homes, where there is rivalry between certain families in purchasing modern furnishings, appliances, and automobiles. Property now brings prestige and is a motivating force behind wage work. The things money can buy have important symbolic value in this prestige system. As we shall see in a later chapter, cooperation still pertains in respect to Shalako and other religious functions, when wealth is "spread around" by lavish entertaining and gift giving. But certain families, especially the stockmen, no longer participate in giving Shalako, which may cost several thousand dollars. While there used to be eight Shalako houses built each year in the last century, now there are never more than six, and sometimes not that many.

The power system also shows evidence of change. The man of property is beginning to be a man of power, taking his place alongside the priests. This is apparent in the rise of the civil government of the pueblos. Thirty years ago, the governor and his council were under the thumb of the caciques. Today they have gained a considerable measure of autonomy. For many years now, the governors have been prosperous stockmen, and for good reason. They are the ones who best understand the white man's way of doing business and are therefore the best qualified to represent the economic interests of the pueblo in dealing with outsiders: the Indian Service, traders, and all others who have an interest or a stake in Zuni wealth.

This new power system has grown up alongside the old system, whereby inherited religious knowledge was the sole fountainhead of power and prestige. To understand fully the over-all change that has taken place, due in part to economic change, it will be essential to gain some understanding of the traditional social organization, religion, and civil government.

CHAPTER 4

CLAN AND KIN

The Clan Today

The total socioreligious structure of Zuni is a most intricate network, with a complexity of structure and function which surpasses that of any other Indian group in the United States. Indeed, it is quite possible that no other single Indian village north of the valley of Mexico had greater complexity in times past. Hopi also has a complex organization, but it is not welded into a single village that dominates the whole, as at Zuni.

The Zuni tribe is divided into thirteen matrilineal clans, which vary in size from a few members to large groups such as Pikchikwe (Dogwood), with several hundred members, consisting of almost a quarter of the total Zuni population. Since Kroeber made his study of the social organization in 1915-16 (Kroeber 1917), two clans have become extinct, while the comparative sizes of the clans have remained very much the same as they were in his day.[34] The principal function of the clans, which are still active at the present day, is the regulation of marriage. In 1947, a sample of 10 per cent of the males under forty years of age revealed only one endogamous marriage within the clan, which was the situation in the early part of the century, when Kroeber also noted one such "incestuous" marriage (Kroeber 1917: 92). The Zuni, man or woman, is also restricted from marrying within the clan of the father, but this rule is not so rigidly adhered to. Many of the larger clans have subdivisions, which are designated by name and whose members may not intermarry. Otherwise, these subdivisions represent unimportant social distinctions in Zuni life (Kroeber 1917: 100-03).

While there is evidence that the clans are not strictly localized within the pueblo, there is a general identification between groups of clans and the quarter of the village in which they reside[35]. When members of the clans living

in the north, south, east, and west quadrants of the village moved out from
the old crowded pueblo, they moved in the same compass direction with
which they were earlier associated. This seems to be as true now as it was
in the early days of the century. [36]

Each clan has a fetish which it cares for. These fetish objects,
ettowe, are highly sacrosanct, and those of the Rain Priests, which are
handed down in certain clan lines, are "of indescribable sanctity, and in
them rests the whole welfare of the people." (Bunzel 1929-30a: 490). The
holding of the most sacred of these ritual properties marks the "important"
families of Zuni, according to the traditional rationale. These particular
lineages (within clan lines) hold the rights to the rituals that go with the fetish
and pass on the offices of priesthood, which have clan identity. Thus the
Priesthood of the North is always a member of Dogwood clan, the Priesthood
of the South, a member of Badger clan. Likewise the Director of the
Kotikan·e (Katchina society) should belong to Deer clan, and other religious
functionaries similarly inherit their office by virtue of clan identity.

In contrast to the Hopi, "Zuni has emphasized household and village
organization at the expense of a strong clan system, whereas the Hopi have
reversed the emphasis" (Eggan 1950: 221). The Zuni clans own no hunting
grounds or agricultural lands. The system of reckoning kin is less rigidly determined by clan and more by other types of association (Eggan 1950: 218).
Nor are there any clan houses or clan "mothers," as among the Hopi. This
development of social relationships which cut in many directions is one of the
features of the social organization that has held Zuni together, while the Hopi
organization, structured more rigidly along clan lines, has been prone to cleavage. Eggan has stated it well (1950:219): "Zuni tradition is throughout concerned with the people as a whole, and in contrast to Hopi legends, scarcely
at all with the fortunes of individual clans."

The household, which is the primary economic unit in Zuni society
(along with the matrilineal lineage or the part thereof that forms the backbone
of such a household), is the connecting link between the individual and his own
clan. Such lineages within the clan are not necessarily closely tied together.
Rather it is into his own constellation of relatives that the individual is born
and from which he receives his primary orientation (Eggan 1950: 188). Such
a household consists of a line of women of successive generations, their husbands (all of other clans), and the children of such married couples. A boy,
when he grows up and marries, will go to live in the house of his wife's mother,
though he frequently comes back to visit his natal household. If his wife dies,
a man will rejoin his clanmates in the house where he was brought up. His
children do not come with him, but stay in the house of the deceased wife, to
whose clan they belong.

While the individual belongs to the clan of his mother, he is the "child of," or "born for," the clan of his father. The obligations to this other lineage and, beyond that, to the clan of which it is a part complement the obligations to one's own clan. The fetishes that give power to the Ashiwanni (Rain Priest) belong to his own (mother's) lineage and clan, but the public enactment of the ritual that goes with the fetish is performed by the Katchina society. His membership in this society is proposed by a male member of the household of his father's sister, thus establishing his identity with this other lineage. There are also numerous private as well as public rituals that serve to link the individual with the father's lineage, many of which take place as part of the crises rites (see Chapter 7 on the life cycle).

A male thus has a close association with three different household groups and the lineages of which they may be a part: (1) that of his sisters and mother (2) that of his father, and (3) that of his wife. For a woman, these identifications and interhousehold associations are much more limited and are centered in her own household, except for relations with her father's relatives. But even here the relationships are attenuated, as the woman has fewer ritual duties and does not (except under extraordinary circumstances), belong to the Katchina cult. Rather than the woman going out to her father's household, as she advances in age, her brother's children come to her. Kroeber expressed it thus (1917: 47-48): "So generation succeeds generation, the slow stream of mothers and daughters forming a current that carried with it husbands, sons, and grandsons."

As a result of this system, the women may very well be more secure (Benedict 1934a: 75-76):

> For women there is no conflict. They have no allegiance
> of any kind to their husbands' groups. But for all men
> there is double allegiance. They are husbands in one
> group and brothers in another. . . Certainly in the more
> important families, in those families which care for per-
> manent fetishes, a man's allegiance as brother has more
> social weight than his allegiance as husband. In all
> families a man's position derives, not, as with us, from
> his position as breadwinner, but from his role in relation
> to the sacred objects of the household.

Residence is not always matrilineal. Sometimes the woman lives in the household of the husband. Kroeber wrote (1917: 92): "I should estimate that from five to ten per cent of Zuni women always flew in the face of propriety to live with their husbands rather than lose them."

Kinship

There has been disagreement among scholars as to the nature of the Zuni kinship system. Fred Eggan (1950: 182), using the earlier data collected by Kroeber (1917), hypothesized that it was not a bilateral system, as Kroeber had advanced. On the contrary, Eggan said, this was a Crow type system in which unilineal descent groups traced through the female line were the basis of the kinship organization. In this system one belonged to only one descent group; no two unilineal descent groups overlap in membership.

According to Eggan, the Crow system at Zuni, like that at Hopi, classified together the father's sister, her daughters, and the women in descending generations. All of these women were called by the same term. In other words, the Zuni (and Hopi) lump together women whom we in Western society would separate out and distinguish as aunt, cousin, niece, grandniece, etc. Men of the father's clan are similarly grouped, crosscutting generation lines. In such a system mother's father and father's father are called by the same term, but there is a separate term for mother's mother and father's mother--in keeping with separating out the female descent groups from each other.

Briefly, other characteristics of the Zuni system are: father and father's brother are classed together; mother and mother's sister are called by the same term. Siblings are distinguished by the same age and sex, younger and older brother and sister by a male speaker, while a female speaker does not distinguish the sex of younger siblings but does for elder siblings.

Parallel cousins are classified with Ego's siblings. But with cross cousins, there are many alternate sets of terms. For example, father's sister's daughter may be called by the same term as father's sister or elder sister, and father's sister's son may be called either "elder brother" or "father."

In recent years there has been a re-examination of the problem by Schneider and Roberts, who collected new data in the field. They have come to the conclusion that the Zuni system is at best a modified Crow type: "One might say that the lineage principle dwindles down at the end of the father's lineage and never gets to the mother's father's lineage" (Schneider and Roberts 1956: 15).

Furthermore: "at crucial points Zuni terminology is equivocal; it is neither clear-cut Crow type nor is it unambiguously generation type by virtue of permitting alternate terms for cross cousins" (Schneider and Roberts 1956: 15).

They agree with Kroeber's statement that the individual Zuni is more interested in the person as such and his status relationship to other persons than
in the logical consistency of the designation following out lineage principles.
  In other words, the genealogical relationships, which are so important at Hopi, here at Zuni are modified by the necessity of role designations
in a society where groupings of many different types cut across kin relations.
As Schneider and Roberts write (1956: 18): "Relative age, affiliation through
ceremonial extension, class affiliations, considerations of courtesy, personal
relationship, and the value of extending kinship as widely as possible all go
along with genealogical position to determine the kinship term applied and
the role played." They are of the opinion that while Zuni must be considered a matrilineal society and not one where kinship is reckoned bilaterally,
the importance of nonkin associations gives an over-all pattern of integration
which is Ego-centered rather than unilineal--as at Hopi, with its strong lineage groups.
  Extensions of kin term usage go beyond family and clan lines. A boy's
ceremonial sponsor in the Katchina cult, his ceremonial father, is called by
the father term. Correspondingly, members of this man's household are also
called by the terms the boy would use in his own family, and the rules of ex-
ogamy apply to the women in such a group as well. The man who initiates a
man or woman into a curing society also becomes a "father," and the same
terminology pertains. The Ashiwanni are called "fathers," and the governor
and his wife are called "father" and "mother." The whole ceremonial life is
pervaded by the concept of kinship. In every ceremony is found the ritual exchange of kinship terms, and the deities are grouped in terms of kinship. The
dead are referred to as "fathers" and "mothers," and the rain clouds may be
thought of as "grandmothers" (Kroeber 1917: 74-75). There are other extensions going further out into the universe:

> Cushing records five things that are necessary to the
> Zuni: the sun "father," the earth "mother," the
> water who is "grandfather," the fire who is "grand-
> mother" and the corn "brothers and sisters" [Parsons
> 1917b: 249 ff.].

Again we see how the world of the supernaturals is tied into conceptual relations
with the workaday associations of kinsmen.

Social Change

  To bring this picture up to date, we can note a few of the changes that
have come about in Zuni clan and kinship behavior since Kroeber and others
were at Zuni. Kroeber himself noted the incipient beginnings of the breakdown

of matrilocal residence. A sample of 10 per cent of the population in 1947 (all veterans) revealed six instances of patrilocality. Furthermore, there is also a growing number of men and women who live independently of either the the mother's or the father's household. One of the more acculturated young men expressed it this way: "It is best to have your own house. Then you can live as you want and do not have to get into quarrels with your wife's family." It so happened that he and his wife did not have their own house, only he wished that they did.

As we have seen in Chapter 3, "breadwinning" carries with it more prestige than it used to. Families that used to be unimportant because of lack of a fetish or ettowe religious office are becoming important in the minds of the younger generation due to their accumulation of economic goods.

Thus, the reciprocal social and religious relationships described in this chapter (and elaborated on in the succeeding chapters) are gradually breaking down, due to the increasing importance given material possessions and the accompanying drift away from matrilocality.

CHAPTER 5

RELIGION

Purposes and Functions

At Zuni, the religious needs of the pueblo as a whole are met by the knowledge and compulsive acts of the priests, accompanied by group ritual, usually in dance form, while the religious needs of the individual are primarily answered by the curers, the members of what Ruth Bunzel has called the cult of the Beast Gods. In order to understand the relationship between the priests, who focus their magic on weather control, crop fertility, and human fecundity, and the curers, it is well to look again at the pueblo's past.

In the Anasazi area, centering around the San Juan river drainage, agriculture developed many centuries ago from what had been a hunting and gathering economy. In all probability the religion of the Pueblo ancestors known to the archaeologists as the "basketmakers" was a shamanistic one, not unlike that found in the rest of aboriginal North America. The shaman received his inspiration directly from the supernaturals. But with the development of agriculture during early pueblo history, it may be argued that this religion, which met the needs of the individual hunters and gatherers, changed to one in which supernatural controls were tailored to the needs of a larger and more closely-knit group. In all probability, new religious forms diffused to this area from Mexico and Central America as part of the total agricultural complex.

The natural control over the crops, i. e. horticultural technology, became buttressed by supernatural techniques essential to agriculturalists in a region of sparse rainfall. These religious techniques became exactly prescribed and tremendously elaborated. They were passed on from one generation to the next by a highly organized system of teaching. The welfare of the crops and the community were at stake; nothing could be left to chance or to the inspiration of a few shamans. The ritual formulas came to be passed down from one generation to the next in family lines. Large group ceremonials grew up. So, in the American Southwest, as in other regions such as the Andean area in South America, Mesopotamia, Egypt, and the Indus river valley, we find that shamanism gives way to priest craft as agriculture develops from the simpler subsistence patterns. North of Mexico, religion of this type was confined to the American Southwest.

But the needs of the individual are still present, as well as those of the group. The twentieth-century Zuni may fall ill and seek help from the curers, just as his ancestors needed the aid of the shaman long ago. Today these curers, who derive their power from the Beast Gods, especially the Bear, perform their magic by learned recipes. Curing, once the province of the inspired shaman, has been modified by the learned behavior of the priests.

Today it is the learning and repetition of religious formulas and ritual that characterize Zuni religion, both the private cure and the public cere- mony. This body of religious knowledge is so tremendous that it can be en- compassed only by the concerted efforts and cooperative endeavors of a whole corps of priests (and curers), who devote their lives to religious duty. At an early age they begin to learn the prayers and rituals, as understudies of the older priests. As the old men die, younger ones take their places, and inherit through clan lines sacred corn bundles, called ettowe. The learning of the prayers must be letter-perfect, the fashioning of the feather prayer sticks just so, and the ritual dances performed in exact fashion, otherwise the gods will bring drought and the crops will fail.

This is a religion of great formalism, precision, and compulsion. Nothing is left in the balance; there is room for free play and individual vari- ation in song, costume, and dance only as secondary features, as embellish- ments to the basic form. This exact ordering of detail seems to be a deep- seated psychological trait manifested in the Rorschach protocols, as we shall see in Part II, and in the art of the Zuni jeweler, whose setting of small tur- quoise in rigid lines has the same monotony of pattern as the dance in the plaza.

In Zuni religion, the gods must be compelled by precise action. Once these ritual acts are performed, they automatically bring the desired results. The organization of the priests and the part each plays in the working whole are as precisely defined as the prayers they utter for the public good. Each of the priests is trained to carry on his own duties, which interlock with those of other priests like the gears of a delicate machine.

Such a religion works in two ways. In order to compel the gods to bring rain, one must also compel one's self to perform the necessary acts and, at the same time, exert pressures on one's fellow men to do likewise. As with other religious systems, the failure to attain the desired goal is explained by man's failure to live up to his bargain with the supernaturals. Drought is caused by

the breaking of religious sanctions: a taboo was violated, a prayer wrongly
uttered, a prayer stick misplaced. Also, such acts may be the work of
witches, fellow men of evil heart working against the commonweal. This
attention to a myriad of religious duties requires extreme control over a man's
life, a system of controls that are inculcated from infancy, first by his immediate family and then, as he grows up, by other social groupings. Discipline is part and parcel of religion, and it is these controls of man over man
as well as of man over the gods that account for the long life of Pueblo culture in a hostile environment.

Religious Techniques

"Practically all the techniques employed by primitive or civilized
man to influence the supernatural are known at Zuni--fetishism, imitative
magic, incantations, and formulae figure largely in ritual" (Bunzel 1929-30a:
489). In the personal religious acts, purification, abstinence, and sacrifice
are also present (Bunzel 1929-30a: 489). Care for sacred objects (fetishism)
is most important, for the whole welfare of the people depends on the proper
treatment of the ettowe. Prayers (formulas) accompany all important religious
occasions; the most vital and powerful of these are uttered by the priests in
retreat from the distractions of mundane affairs. The repeated formulas give
efficacy to the dances and songs that are performed in public.
 Offerings to the gods play a considerable part in Zuni religious life.
Food, tobacco, prayer meal (made of ground corn, shell, and turquoise), and
prayer sticks decorated with feathers are essential and accompany both public
ceremonials and devotions in the home. After each meal a devout Zuni places
to one side a bit of food as an offering to the gods.
 In addition to the religious acts described above, there are taboos of
many kinds. Certain foods may not be mixed together; others are prohibited
on certain occasions to members of particular religious societies. Shrines and
rooms where sacred objects are kept are surrounded by restrictions. The behavior of men in office is rigidly prescribed, as are the actions of others toward
them when they are performing their religious rites. The breaking of such
taboos brings the displeasure of the gods to the transgressor and, if serious, may
even affect the whole village.
 Purification, or ritual cleansing, is also important in all ceremonies.
The washing of the hair in yucca suds is perhaps the most noteworthy; the suds
of the yucca billow up like clouds and thus compel the rain to fall. Whipping
accompanies certain rituals, not to punish but to purify, for by such means evil
is driven out.

All these techniques are basic to most ceremonies, which vary in details of prayer, songs, and dance. There is room for some variation and aesthetic expression in the composition of the song to be sung or the dance to be performed. However, it is expression to which the whole performing group agrees, and it is presented as the creation of the group rather than the accomplishment of the individuals.

Structure of Religious Groupings

The structure of the religious organization is as intricate as the ritual it perpetuates. It consists of numerous cult groups, each with its own set of secrets and accompanying power. It must never be forgotten that, in Pueblo rationale, power is invested in secrecy itself. A secret shared with others not initiated into the particular cult (and this of course applies to the Zuni uninitiated as well as the white man or other outsider) is power lost. The efficacy of closely guarded knowledge is a basic Pueblo law, and violation is the supreme crime.

The cult with the greatest concentration of powerful knowledge is that of the Rain Priests, the Ashiwanni. There are twelve such priests, and of these, four are more sacred than the others. These four are equated with the cardinal directions, and the Priest of the North rules over all. He is the "house chief," the Kakwemosi. These four priests were the focus of political and religious power in the old days. They and their assistants, along with the Pekwin (Sun Priest) and the two head Bow Priests (leaders of the War cult) comprised a council of priests that looked to the religious needs of the people. They selected those who were to impersonate the gods in the great annual ritual, Shalako. They also ordered the events in the religious calendar and met on occasions of tribal calamity.

The Bow Priests were the "defenders and the executive arm of the religious hierarchy" (Bunzel 1929-30a: 526). It was up to them to carry out the decrees of the council of priests. If the Rain Priests themselves were to enforce the law, they might become involved in the quarrels and violence which, in Zuni belief, would drive away the clouds and bring drought and starvation to the village.

The religious structure consists of five other groups in addition to that of the Rain Priests. Ruth Bunzel, who has made the most careful study of Zuni religion as it is practiced in the twentieth century, calls these groupings "cults." Each is a secret society with its own esoteric set of beliefs and rituals known only to a select number who have undergone initiation rites. These five cults are described below (Bunzel 1929-30a: 511):

(1) The cult of the Sun is led by the Pekwin, one of the most holy priests. It is his duty to watch the sun, keep it on its course, and set the date for Shalako.

He sets up the altars for ceremonies and installs new priests, including the Bow Priests. The sun is thought of as the source of all life, and the devout Zuni greets him each morning with prayer. The Pekwin "is ultimately held responsible for the welfare of the community" (Bunzel 1929-30a: 512), and as such is a leader of the people as well as of the priests.

(2) The Katchina cult[37] is best known to the outsider, for the Zuni, along with the Hopi, still permit visitors to watch their ritual masked dances. All adult males belong to this organization, which is in reality a tribal society. Women belong only under extraordinary circumstances. The society is organized into six divisions, identified with the four cardinal points, the zenith, and the nadir. Each of these six groups has its own ceremonial house, or kiva, and, in turn, each of the kivas has its own officers, who set the dates for dances and recruit members to take part in them. Each kiva has many more members than will turn up for any particular dance. Membership in the kiva group is determined shortly after birth, when the male child's ceremonial father is selected from the household of the father's sister. This ceremonial father will sponsor the child when as a young boy he is formally initiated into the tribal cult.

The dances given by these kiva groups are elaborate rituals, demanding many rehearsals in the kiva, where songs are composed and costumes planned prior to the public performance in the plaza. There, during the summer afternoons, the women and children take their places on the edge of the plaza to watch the dance, listen to the songs, and enjoy the antics of the clowns. In the evening the crowd grows as the men returning to the village from their work in the cornfields stop off to watch the dance before going home for supper.

During recent years there has been a tendency to perform the dances over the weekend, when kiva members who work for wages are free to participate (Bunzel 1929-30b: 848).

(3) The cult of the Katchina Priests is essentially a cult within a cult.[38] However, Bunzel treats it separately from the Katchina cult proper, even though there are close associations between the two groups. The primary concern of the Katchina Priests is human rather than crop fertility; they play a central part in the annual Shalako. The masks of the impersonators of the Katchina Priests are tribally owned rather than individually owned and, like the ettowe, they are carefully guarded and "fed" and are kept in the custody of certain lineages. All of the past impersonators of these central roles in the Shalako ceremony form a cult group which alone knows the secrets of that particular ritual performance, and it is they who select the next impersonators.

The season of greatest activity for the Katchina Priests is at the great house-blessing ceremony given during the early winter. Then these priests accompany the Messengers of the Gods, known as Shalako (and for whom the ceremony is named) during their night of ritual dancing in newly-erected houses.

To this group also belong the koyemshi, the sacred clowns. According to the origin myth, they are the fruit of an incestuous union. They participate in ceremonies the year round, amuse the crowds between "sets" at the summer dances, and have an important part in Shalako. While they are greatly loved by the people, they are also greatly feared, for they have power which can be used malevolently. To deny a koyemshi food when he makes his collecting round of the village is to court disaster.

(4) Membership in the cult of the War Gods today (1947) is limited to one man. In earlier days, when the Zuni engaged in active warfare, this cult was led by the Elder Brother Bow Priest, assisted by the Younger Brother Bow Priest. They obtained their power directly from the Ahayuta, the twin children of the sun, who figure in the origin legend as the war leaders who led the Zuni to victory over the enemy. This cult controlled the war rituals which overcame the enemy, and it was mandatory for any warrior who had taken scalps to join this society, for if he did not, "ghost illness" would spread through the village. Induction into the society was accomplished by a scalp dance wherein the scalp of an enemy was placed on a pole around which everyone danced. The potential malevolence of the enemy ghost was transformed into a positive good. Through ritual compulsion, the scalp became a rain fetish, and henceforth was kept in a special house guarded and treated by the Scalp Priest, one of the initiated members of the War cult.

External warfare waged against the enemy was not the only duty of the Bow Priests and the other initiates. They also waged internal warfare, for, as mentioned above, they were the executive arm of the high priests who enforced religious "law." Another duty was to guard the secrets of the various cult groups to which their members were assigned as protectors. In addition, the Bow Priests were responsible for the seeking out of witches, who used malevolent powers to bring wind, drought, and illness to the village.

Cushing was initiated into this cult, and was able to witness and participate in rituals of many cult groups. In his day, the Bow Priests still had great authority and were, as he describes it, much feared:

> like a vigilance committee, the priesthood of the
> Bow secretly tries all cases of capital crime under
> the name of sorcery or witchcraft--the war-chief
> of the nation, himself necessarily a prominent
> priest of the Bow, acting as executioner, and, with
> the aid of his subchiefs, as secretly disposing of the
> body. On account of this mysterious method of
> justice, crime is rare in Zuni [Cushing 1882-83:
> 26, 44].

The central position of these Bow Priests in maintaining village control in the

name of the council of high priests is well symbolized by their roles as con-
veyors of the cane of office to the governor and members of his council.
They also collected the canes upon impeachment of a governor.

(5) The final cult to be considered is the cult of the Beast Gods, which
consists of a group of twelve curing societies, or fraternities, as they are
called in the earlier literature. These societies, open to both men and
women, derive their power from the Beast Gods, animals of prey. These gods
are the source of disease and of death, which is believed to be transmitted by
witches. They are also the givers of medicines and magical powers, which
can be used by members of the curing societies to neutralize the actions of
the witches. Each of the different curing cults has its own specialties: one
society treats bullet wounds, another sore throats, another victims of lightning.
Others may treat cases of difficult childbirth, epilepsy, etc. In addition to
these specialties, all of the societies practice "general medicine," which, in
effect, is exorcism of witches. If an individual is seriously ill and his life is
in danger he may be "given" to a society. If the cure is successful, he may
be initiated into the organization which saved him--if he can afford the initiation fee. This is to make the cure permanent and to safeguard the secrets that
he has witnessed in the course of his own cure. Each society is divided into
two orders, made up of those who know the full curing rites and those appren-
tices who may someday attain the higher order. In several of the societies
there are also fire-eating, stick-swallowing, and juggling suborders, whose
performances are directed to weather control. Today many of these activities
are either extinct or exist in a very attenuated form.

The activities of all these diverse cults dovetail in one ceremony:
Shalako, the house-blessing ceremony, which is performed each year at the
return of the winter solstice. Each year, new impersonators are selected to
play the role of the Shalako, the Messengers of the Gods, the giant masked
figures who come to bless six new (or reconstructed) houses. Certain of the
Katchina Priests are also selected annually to utter their prayers on Shalako
night. The koyemshi, the leaders of the curing societies, and the kiva groups
all participate in this elaborate religious festival, which may well be the most
complex of all religious ceremonies still performed in North America. It
comes as the culmination of many months of intense activity of the Shalako,
the koyemshi, and the other impersonators of the gods who take part in the
building of the new houses constructed for and at the expense of the families
who elect to have their homes so blessed and honored by the gods. Such
sponsorship costs thousands of dollars. The builders must be fed while the
construction is underway, and the large crowd of Indians from the other pueblos,
Navahos, and Anglos who come to Zuni on the night when the Messengers of
the Gods dance for the people must be provided for. Shalako remains a flour-
ishing institution. Although there are only six and sometimes only five houses

constructed, the ceremony is full and rich. The costumes, dances, and prayers show little signs of decay. Shalako attests to the still vigorous religious life of the Zuni people.

Religious Change

Complete data are not available on changes in the religious organization and its functioning. It would be of considerable interest to the ethnologist if a complete census could be taken of the membership and of the degree of participation of each member in the curing societies and in the kiva dance groups. Comparison of such data with that collected by Kroeber and Parsons thirty-five years ago would give valuable indications of religious change in the face of rapid acculturation to American society. A careful reading of the materials of the earlier ethnologists does give a picture of disintegration in certain parts of the religious structure: stick-swallowers perform at very infrequent intervals; certain large ceremonies such as the Scalp Dance likewise occur only at long intervals; it is difficult to get participation of the younger women in the dance for the Santo; kick-stick races were not held in 1947; the communal rabbit hunts are less frequent. By 1952 the office of the Sun Priest had no incumbent, while the former Pekwin took up residence in Gallup. These are details of some importance to the ethnographer, but the general trend will suffice for our present purpose.

During the years immediately following the war, certain ceremonies were revived that had not been held in many years. This was part of what may be thought of as a nativistic reaction, which set in during the early 1940s. In part it was a reaction to losing 10 per cent of the total population (50 per cent of the males between 18 and 38) to the war effort. Although the young priests were deferred from the draft through pressure of the council of priests, there was great concern as to how the religion could be carried on with so many men away. These men, in the opinion of the older priests, should have been learning the ways of their elders and participating in the Katchina cult. When they came back from the service there was a burst of religious activity. Great pressure was exercised to get new inductees into the medicine societies and to obtain new Bow Priests from among those veterans who were now qualified to join the War cult. It was this nativistic reaction that brought about a revival of certain ceremonies. As Parsons puts it: "The ceremony that has lapsed at Zuni is never quite as dead as it may seem" (Parsons 1939: 2, 881).

In all likelihood there will continue to be other revivals of old customs, old ceremonies, etc., but still the disintegration will go on, for it is becoming increasingly difficult for families to force the young men who have been brought up in modern schools and who for some years may have lived away from the pueblo to devote their lives to ritual and prayer. In the last century there were no alternatives facing these young priests. There was only one way of life and one system of values.

The older people are not in conflict as much as the middle-aged and younger men and women. These younger people show the results of several generations of concerted educational endeavor exerted by Indian Service and missionaries. The young men born into the families in which religious office is handed down are torn between the old way of life and the new way: devoting a lifetime to religion or working for cash which will enable the purchase of material goods. As we shall see in the next chapter, there is a growing secularization--religion does not permeate the whole of life as it used to.

Another problem: Is there any evidence of a change in religious values which might lead to a change in ceremony and overt religious activity in the future? The evidence is far from complete, but there is an indication that this may be taking place. Extended interviews with a group of very acculturated veteran informants revealed attitudes which cannot be represented as typical of Zuni opinion but which may point the way to a new ideology. At least three of these young men, when asked if they thought that the Katchina dancers brought rain, vigorously denied that there was any connection between the two. "Dancing doesn't have anything to do with rain," one informant replied. He and other informants gave a scientific explanation that they had read in books or heard in school--and believed. These same veterans said that they took part in the dances to please their families and "to keep the gossip down." Some also enjoyed the feeling of group participation and recreation, while others did not.

But these same men did not have a negative attitude toward curing rituals. One spoke with feeling and admiration of a curer who had removed a thorn from his foot ("shot" there by a witch). "Gee, he sure is a smart man," he said. Similar reactions to the curers were obtained from several other young informants. One fellow, about twenty-eight years of age, said he would probably join a medicine society some day, yet he never took part in rain dances. Why should there no longer be faith in one set of supernatural beliefs and a reaffirmation in another?

There would appear to be several reasons for this. The young people are no longer dependent on raising crops in order to gain a livelihood. A whole generation has passed since the young, as well as the old, were dependent on their fields for their food. Many now prefer to earn cash and buy their food. Once the need is no longer felt, the overt behavior may change. This was exactly why the War cult died out once the need for warriors and the scalp ceremony had passed (Parsons 1939: 2, 1128). If you no longer have religious conviction, why dance in the hot sun? It is easier to work in town or sit in the house and make silver jewelry. We may postulate that when the present generation grows to maturity and the point of view expressed above becomes more prevalent, the general anxiety of the group over weather control will be greatly decreased. The traditional overt manifestation of this feeling of anxiety--group ceremonials--will likewise decrease. On the other hand, while the general or group problem of village survival in the face of drought may disappear, the Zuni may find a new source of anxiety in the many individual problems besetting members of a rapidly changing culture. This anxiety may seek religious relief in an increased reliance on the activities of the curing societies. The curer relieves feelings of uncertainty and insecurity for the individual, just as the Katchina Priest and those who give him power relieve anxiety on the group level. Certainly anxiety is increasingly present in a rapidly changing world in which one has to make choices where before no alternatives existed. The individual anxieties patterned by the culture are projected on to others who are believed to be witches.[39] It is this anxiety that the shaman relieves when he "sucks out" the object shot into the patient by a witch.

Such a prognosis seems to "fit" when we review the trend in certain of the other pueblos, where individualization and secularization are much further developed as a result of a longer period of acculturation. At Isleta, curing ceremonies appear to be of greater moment than fertility ceremonies. The same is also true at Laguna and possibly at Santa Clara. So, too, have these "negative" aspects of religion, witchcraft for example, outlived the more positive aspects. This is well illustrated in West African society and in other world areas. The sorcerer and the shaman outlive the priest.

CHAPTER 6

CIVIL GOVERNMENT: THE SEPARATION OF STATE FROM CHURCH

There is some question as to the existence of a civil government at
Zuni before the conquest. Some historians state that the governor and his
helpers were introduced into the pueblos by the Spanish authorities, who real-
ized the need of an intermediary between affairs of the external world and
the self-contained theocracy. Cushing reported in the 1880s that the two Bow
Priests[40] appointed the governor and lieutenant governor, who in turn selected
their assistants, the tenientes (Cushing 1882). The position of the Bow Priests,
the executive arm of the council of priests, was central to the whole system
of civil government. But it must be remembered that these Bow Priests were
deputies of the council and, as such, simply kept order within the pueblo and
waged war on external enemies. It was the Bow Priests who made it possible
for the Ashiwanni and the Pekwin to concentrate on their prayers and remain
aloof from mundane political affairs. This was important, for, as we have
noted before, a strong Zuni belief even today is that if the priests become involved in politics this will lead to quarrels which will offend the gods and
bring drought. Furthermore, the Bow Priests and the civil governors whom
they appointed provided a double wall between the council of priests and the
outside world. During the Spanish, the Mexican, and the American territorial
periods, outsiders first met the governors, who had little or no religious sanctity, then the Bow Priests, who stood behind them. The secrets, fetishes, and
rituals of the priestly bodies were well hidden from view.

About the turn of the century, the system changed. This change was
probably due to the lapse in power and membership of the War cult, led by the
Bow Priests. Without doubt the prestige of this group suffered when wars with
the Navaho and Apache came to an end. Recruitment to this cult slackened
when it became increasingly difficult to obtain the requisite enemy scalps. The
cult no longer held the central executive position that it once had, and by the
early 1900s the council of priests, rather than the Bow Priests, were appointing

the governor and the other civil officers.[41] They were now brought into direct contact with political matters, a contact which has contributed to political disturbance in the pueblo ever since.

In 1917, when Parsons witnessed the installation of the governor, his appointment was made only after the priests had canvassed the village to find someone who would accept the position. At that time the civil officers were not changed at regular two-year intervals, as they are now, and they often remained in office for as long as five years if they held the favor of the people and the priests. Once the governor, his lieutenant, and the tenientes had been selected, they were installed in office at a public ceremony held in the dance plaza. At this ceremony the outgoing officers handed over their badges of office, the canes, to the new incumbents. Thus the people ratified the change of officers, and the ritual essential to any important Zuni function was duly performed. Without the passing on of the cane to the governor he is not installed.[42] It is as if the source of his power came from the cane itself, just as in Zuni belief the source of the Rain Priests' power is in their fetishes.[43]

During the early 1920s, the populace split into two separate political factions over disagreement as to whether the Catholic church should be readmitted to the pueblo as a mission group. The Catholic church was readmitted, but, according to Parsons, not without the help of the government agent, who was a Catholic. This split into pro-Catholic and anti-Catholic factions also brought about a cleavage among the priests. Now that they were appointing the civil government directly, the priests were in the middle of politics.

Starting around 1924 and lasting up to 1935, there was growing difficulty in getting the civil government installed. The priests could not agree as to suitable candidates. It may be presumed that some wanted to keep Catholic sympathizers out, while others welcomed them.[44] This is no doubt an oversimplification of a complex factional dispute that requires an intimate knowledge of the pueblo in those years for full understanding. The dispute also involved the traders, missionaries, and government workers. In 1924 and again in 1926, the priests could not agree as to the choice for governor, and two sets of officers were chosen. Finally they chose one man, who served for seven years.

Serious trouble again occurred in 1934, when the cane of the new governor, a member of a pro-Catholic family, was taken back by the priests while he was away on a hunting trip. As a result of all this difficulty, the subagent suggested that the Zuni select a lay nominating committee, which would choose a panel of nominees for each of the civil offices. These would then be voted upon by the people in public meeting. The subagent thought that in order for the panel to remain impartial to the political camps in the village there should be three members on the committee from the Catholic faction and three from the non-Catholic or Protestant group. This new system was accepted by the Zuni.

The subagent had resorted to action which set up an intermediary body between the high priests and the civil governors, i.e. it replaced the now defunct Bow Priests. Although the times had changed, the council of priests resented being deprived of their prerogative. The nominating committee, which was dominated by returned boarding school students, represented a progressive faction in the pueblo, and it may be inferred that it went along with the Indian Service on many policies. It was also a group of politically able men--three of the original six members of the committee have held the governorship at different times since 1935.

At the present time the civil officers consist of: the governor, or tapup, as he is known to the Zuni; the lieutenant governor, called sipaloa[45] shiwanni (Mexican priest); and six tenientes. Of the tenientes, two are chosen from Zuni, two from Nutria, one from Pescado, and one from Ojo Caliente. The governor, assisted by his officers, is responsible for all public works and programs that lie outside of the religious sphere. He calls out the men of the pueblo for the annual ditch cleaning in the Zuni valley, and the local tenientes do the same in the farming villages. Matters affecting grazing regulations, livestock sales, public utilities (water, and more recently Rural Electrification Administration), and school matters (including delinquency and truancy), all fall to him and his officers. Maintaining public law and order is also one of his functions. Assisted by the Indian police (paid from tribal funds) he must enforce the liquor law, especially at Shalako time, when bootlegging prevails. He hears cases with the council and pronounces sentence; fines go into the tribal treasury. The governor also hears and adjudicates quarrels over land ownership and disputes between families, including property settlements at the time of divorce.

His job is a heavy one. One of the recent subagents remarked: "The Zunis work their governors to death." The demands on his time are so heavy that he frequently calls for assistance from the village at large to get in his crop. This assistance, transcending the more limited family, lineage, and clan obligations, is further evidence of growing secularization. A hundred years ago only a high priest such as the Kakwemosi (Priest of the North) could demand such aid, and then only when he was involved in religious duty. The governor's job is not a popular one, not only because of the amount of work involved but because the governor must arbitrate in disputes and make direct demands of individuals, who may take offense. As Bunzel says (1929-30a: 480): "The thing a Zuni will avoid above anything else is giving offense." Underlying this is probably the deep-seated fear of witch powers used by "those jealous ones." With little doubt, such fears have been a concern of many governors in the past.

In 1943 the most serious political trouble of all flared up, leading to a crisis which was quite possibly the greatest in the memory of Zuni. This is not the place to review the event in detail. In brief it may be stated that the governor was impeached for trying to advance his own wishes by misrepresenting a paper signed by the council of priests (who could not read). The priests had believed that by signing the paper they would keep the young Zuni men from being drafted. In reality, the signed document asked for the removal of an Indian Service employee of many years' tenure, who had recently been appointed acting subagent. This employee, a Spanish-American, had served at Zuni with no difficulty up to that time. Now the governor, his sworn enemy of many years' standing (as it came out in the investigation that followed), wanted to have him removed from the office of subagent. The governor and the priests vouched (in the misrepresented paper) that the man would be offensive to the Zuni people as a subagent, in that he would have to make certain inquiries into religious matters held absolutely secret from Spanish-Americans. This paper was sent to a high official in Washington. After the impeachment, the lieutenant governor was placed in the governor's vacant office. Then the Sun Priest, who was a political ally of the ex-governor, said that he would not carry on his religious duties unless the impeached governor was reinstalled.

In an attempt to straighten out the matter, the United Pueblos Agency called several meetings. So grave was the mix-up that on those occasions the priests broke precedent and discussed their troubles with the people. According to the report, women sitting in the back of the room cried aloud. After this crisis the high priests asked that the nominating committee be abolished and that the old system, under which they selected the governor, be re-established. This was never done. These conflicts at Zuni led the former Superintendent of the United Pueblos, Dr. Sophie Aberle, to write (Aberle 1948: 64 ff.):

> Most of the pueblos which have changed or are chang-
> ing from the old to the more modern pattern of civil
> organization are functioning relatively well, except
> Zuni. Zuni in 1943 not only had an amorphous civil
> organization, but those in authority were making no
> satisfactory adjustment to changing economic values.
> This status within the tribe was due in large part to a
> lack of experience of the pueblo in handling their own
> government, due to strong paternalistic Federal con-
> trol of the civil affairs of the group up until 1935.

No doubt paternalism has impeded the development of strong civil government at Zuni. But it seems that Aberle failed to make due allowance for the rapid economic growth which had taken place at Zuni and the concomitant change in the power system from theocratic to secular control over village affairs. The latter has lagged behind economic change. As was pointed out in Chapter 3, this growth has come about more rapidly than in Laguna or the Rio Grande pueblos, where acculturation has been under way for a longer period of time.

However, Aberle does put her finger on one of the major difficulties in the civil governing process. At Zuni, in contrast to the eastern pueblos, there is no body of past officials, e. g. the principales, who meet in council with the governor, lieutenant governor, and tenientes. In the other pueblos, past officials review their experiences with the novice leaders and give a stability to practice and policy which is lacking at Zuni. At Zuni, there is no larger body to guide or act as a sounding board for the governor, who must still resort to public meetings for ratification of his program.

In summary, we find that the strengthening of the civil government represents the rise of a new power system, i. e. a separation of church and state. With this change, Zuni government more closely approximates that of the greater American society. The numerous conflicts in Zuni political life may be viewed as a difference in values between the traditionalists and those men who have been successful in keeping abreast of economic and social change.

CHAPTER 7

LIFE CYCLE

The preceding chapters have dealt with the organization and function
of Zuni society and with some of the changes that it has undergone. There
remains for consideration the experiences of the individual as he enters and
grows up to take part in the society. Since the book so far has described
chiefly the activities of adults, the emphasis here will be upon children and
adolescents.

Pregnancy and Childbirth

A fundamental Zuni system of reasoning--based on the assumption
that like causes like--is resorted to during pregnancy. The expectant mother
and her spouse are restricted in their behavior: all aspects of death must be
avoided, or the fetus will be killed; the wife may not look upon a dead person; her husband may not hunt for wild animals. In the belief of the elders,
a child may be endangered even by the slaughtering of a sheep or a pig.[46] But
actual behavior does not always conform to belief, and farm animals are
killed by some at this time. If the woman mixes different kinds of meat dishes
at the same meal, e.g. venison with mutton or pork with beef, she will have
twins. Twins bring bad luck, and care is taken to avoid giving birth to them.
The mother must not eat rich and fatty foods such as piñon nuts, or her child
will be too large. If a male child is wanted, boys of the household are permitted to be present in the room during delivery, whereas girls may be there if
a female child is desired. They are not permitted to see the actual act of birth,
however, which is screened from them by blankets held up around the mother.
At birth, a midwife who is a member of one of the curing societies is
called in to assist with the delivery. There are four or five such women in the
village, who deliver children according to traditional ways. Other women are
also present, residents of the house who are members of the lineage of the

woman giving birth, i.e. her own mother and sisters. In addition, women come over from the household of the father--his mother plays a most important role in the first days of the baby's life. So we find that at birth itself the child is drawn into a relationship with two clans and two lineages within these clans, that of the mother's mother and that of the father's mother. As noted in an earlier chapter, relationship to the latter is especially important for the male child in ritual obligations.

The woman in childbirth kneels while the midwife stands behind and presses on her abdomen. Soon after birth the newborn child, if a boy, is symbolically initiated into the ritual life of the village by one of the women from the father's household. She touches the child and thereby pledges him to the kiva of her husband.

The care of the child during the first hours of life usually falls to the father's mother. She cuts the navel cord and daubs it with raw fat and unbaked bread dough. According to one informant, when the cord dries up and falls off the navel is treated by rubbing it with dirt from the doorstep. This dirt will keep the navel shut, as it has been trod on by so many feet. Compulsive magic determines the disposal of the cord: that of a girl is buried under a grinding stone, where she must spend many hours grinding corn as a mature woman; that of a boy is buried in the corn field, where he must till the crops.

The woman in attendance shapes the baby's nose and head, pulls its legs and arms to give them proper shape, and prepares the bed on which the mother and child are to spend the next eight days. This is a bed of sand spread out on the floor and heated with hot rocks. Covered with blankets, the mother lies face down on this bed, with a warm stone under her abdomen. The infant is placed beside her. The warmth of the bed on the breasts is believed to start the milk flowing. A perfect ear of corn is placed alongside the child to ward off witches who might attempt to harm him. The baby is rubbed with the fine white powder of wood ashes; so treated the child will never be blemished by the growth of ugly body hair.

In the old days, women observed such a lying-in period for eight days, attended the whole time by either the father's mother or sister. On the fourth and the eighth day the mother and child were bathed; each time the baby was powdered once more with wood ashes. After the bath on the eighth day, the baby was placed on a cradleboard with the ear of corn and taken outdoors. The woman in attendance placed corn meal in the baby's hand and, facing east, uttered a prayer to the rising sun which ended with these words:

> In your thoughts (may we live)
> May we be the ones whom your thoughts
>   will embrace,
> For this, on this day
> To our sun father.

We offer prayer meal.
To this end:
May you help us all to finish our roads
[Bunzel 1929-30d: 636].

These customs are changing, and in increasing numbers the women
are going to the government hospital at Black Rock for their deliveries.
Others prefer to have their babies at home with the doctor and nurse in attendance; still others just call in the field nurse. Some of the people hold
out against the hospital for the reasons expressed by one Zuni father:

M_____ did not go to the hospital to have P____,
although she had the flu when she was pregnant
with him. If Indians are not born in the Indian
way, they get poor and skinny and some get T.B.
At the hospital they don't have hot sand for the
baby and the mother to lie on and they don't have
juniper tea but cold water to drink right after the
baby is born. That spoils the baby and the mother.

On another occasion he said: "Some Zuni want to be like white folks and don't
follow the old ways, then something goes wrong with them" (Stewart 1940-41).

Infancy and Early Childhood

The newborn child is given the breast right after the sand bed has been
prepared, and is allowed to suck even if the mother's milk has not yet come.
If the milk does not run for several days, a woman from the mother's household who has a nursing child acts as wet nurse until the mother can take over.

The cradleboard is usually made for the child by the father. When
the baby is placed on the board, a cloth is put across the chest and under both
arms. Over this a blanket is wrapped. Sometimes a dress may be put on the
child, and more often diapers. Those less affluent use soft rags instead of
diapers. The babies are wrapped with their arms straight alongside the body.
Most children are taken off the board three or four times during the day and
placed on the parents' bed, where they are allowed to kick and exercise. During the daytime, if the child is left alone in the room, it is protected by an
ear of corn left beside it. At night the baby, strapped to the board, is placed
by the mother, who sleeps with her husband on a double bed. There seems to
be a good deal of variation in the length of time babies are kept on cradle-
boards. Some of the more progressive mothers take their children off when
they are only a month or two old, while others use the board for four months
or more; the most conservative mothers may keep their babies strapped to the
board for as long as a year and a half. A Zuni father said that young babies
cry a lot more when they are not on these boards than when they are.

As noted above, the child is protected from witches from the first day of his life; there is little doubt that the adults' fear of witchcraft is conveyed to the child at an early age. Turquoise and flint are placed in the cradle for protection; the first time the child is taken out at night, charcoal is rubbed over his heart so that it will be invisible to any witches who might seek him out as a target for their poisoned missiles. Some parents will not leave a baby alone in a room for fear that a witch might steal it and induct the infant into the witch society. One Zuni father says:

> It is not safe for anyone who is not a relative to
> see a baby. It is not good to want to look at a
> baby who is not in the family, and the parents
> of the child would be suspicious of nonrelatives.
> Even if a mother took her child to the store, she
> would not like it if someone she did not know very
> well, or who was not related, asked to hold her
> child. Because of this fear of witches young chil-
> dren are not taken out of the house very much.

An old Zuni woman recalls the fears of her children:

> All [my children] were a little afraid at night.
> L_____ seemed to be more afraid than the others.
> When the children would go to bed alone in a
> dark room L_____ would start to cry after awhile,
> and I would have to go and lie down with her un-
> til she went to sleep. When asked why she cried
> at night L_____ would say she was afraid of ghosts
> and witches. When she would cry going to bed I
> would scold her, but lie down with her anyway.

It is easy to understand why the Zuni adult is so afraid of being alone at night when we look into the early training of the child. Another woman says:

> I am afraid if I am alone at night because ghosts
> and witches may be around. My mother is afraid
> too. When my daughter was about six I was afraid
> to stay alone with my children when the big boys
> and my husband were away. I asked my father or
> brother or sister to stay with us. Sometimes I stayed
> alone with the children and we put beds together, or
> slept in one bed on the floor. My sister is brave. She
> will stay alone with her children at Pescado. There
> are a few brave women like that, but most Zuni are
> afraid. If I were alone I would keep a lamp burning
> all night. If dogs bark Zuni don't say anything to
> to them because maybe a witch is coming. They

will chase them away. I tell my children to be
quiet and go to sleep at night or else ghosts or
witches will get them. I just do that to scare
them [Stewart 1940-41].

However, the fear of ghosts and witches results in the mother keeping
the child in close proximity, thus giving the infant a sense of security which
later extends to other members of the household. We may find here one
causative agent which tends to dichotomize the behavior of the individual
from an early age; toward the individual's household group there are mutual
feelings of warmth and security, but toward the outsider not related by the
bonds of kinship, the Zuni is taught to behave with caution and circumspec-
tion. These observations of the anthropologists are confirmed by the emotional response tests given by the psychologists. See Part II, Chapter 10.

Babies are nursed whenever they cry; at least this is the ideal pattern--
mothers say that a baby should be fed when it cries and should not be forced
to wait for its feeding. Data on actual practice are lacking.

There is considerable variation in the age at which children are weaned
from the breast. Some mothers nurse their children for only a year, while
others continue nursing their babies until they are two or three years old. The
major determinant seems to be whether or not the mother becomes pregnant
again, in which case the baby is weaned. The transition from the breast is
made easier today by bottles, which the younger mothers have learned to use.
The field nurse has had a great influence on many of the younger women, who
take their children to the well-baby clinic where they are instructed in modern
methods of child care. But several traditional methods of weaning are still
practiced today. Ground chili is placed on the mother's nipple; some mothers
are said to frighten their children by placing small worms on the breast. One
mother reports that her sister told her three-year-old child that Atoshle (the
scare Katchina) would get her if she did not stop sucking her breast.

As the mother's next pregnancy advances, she turns over the care of
her youngest child, who may not be completely weaned as yet, to one of the
other women living in the house--usually her mother or one of her sisters.
This mother surrogate permits the crying child to suck at her own breast and
takes the infant to bed with her at night. This woman also feeds the child its
first solid food, as its own mother is preoccupied with the new arrival. Such
food may be bread soaked in soup or corn meal; "'most anything soft" the
women say.

Later, when the children are old enough to reach for food, they are allowed to eat anything that is on the table, melons and coffee included. When
the stews are too highly seasoned, a separate pot is made for the young child,
but as he grows older he learns to enjoy the taste of chili and eats it with great
relish. As the child grows the parents discourage the wasting of food. In the

words of one adult:

> If kids don't eat what they have, they are told to
> leave the table. Corn is the main thing they are
> not supposed to waste. They say: "corn will cry
> if you leave it outside." Zuni say that if food is
> wasted, we will be hungry [Stewart 1940-41].

No concerted effort is made to toilet train children until they have
been walking for some months. When questioned about how his son had been
trained, one young father reported:

> When P____ was about a year and a half old I
> noticed that he had started to soil the floor [prior
> to this the child had worn diapers]. His mother
> would then take him outside the door and tell
> him to squat and show him how to do it. For a
> couple of months after he had learned to walk he
> would just squat in the house but we would send
> him outside or take him. After that he started
> going by himself. Last week when he soiled over
> in mother's house I scolded him. I just said, "Why
> didn't you go outside?" We scolded him just a little.
> Kids are never spanked for that [Stewart 1940-41].

When the children are older they are taught not to defecate in the yard but to
use the outhouse, which stands at the rear of the Zuni home. Today many
Zuni women keep diapers on their infants when they are off the cradleboard.
The children continue to wear these part of each day until they are toilet
trained. Frequently the children play with their stools, and for this they are
scolded.

The parents have considerably more success training the children to
correct toilet habits during the daytime than at night. Bed-wetting is a frequent occurrence in most households and may continue until the children are
as old as eleven or twelve.

The children in a Zuni household are not put to bed at any certain time,
but are allowed to stay up until they get sleepy; nor are they forced to take naps.
During the winter they are taken to the night dances performed in the houses and
may be seen asleep on their parents' laps when they are too tired to keep their
eyes open. At home the older children may sit up to hear their parents con-
verse; when they are tired they fall asleep on top of the bed with their clothes
on. Several siblings sleep in the same bed together, often with an older member of the household as well. The child is usually well along in adolescence
before he or she is given a bed of his own. The children follow the custom of
the elders; they sleep late in the morning. But of course during most of the
year the older children must be awakened early in order to get to school on

time. In the old days, during both winter and summer the boys were forced to run down to the river and bathe each day before the morning meal.

Later Childhood

As the children grow up they are given various chores around the house. One of the first tasks assigned to both boys and girls is to carry wood for the stove and fireplace. When a boy is about eight years old he is asked to help his father chop wood as well as haul it, which means going out to the forest in the family truck.

At about nine years of age the boys help hoe the corn fields and take part in the planting. Also, the boys are sent out to sheep camp to accompany the older men--their brothers, uncles, or fathers. During these years they do numerous small chores, but their principal value is in companionship to break the monotony of the long hours of herding. Unlike the Navaho, the girls never take part in sheep activities, even as women. As the boys grow older they are given more responsibility in the herding activities, but it is not until they are well along in their teens that they take the sheep out by themselves. They are rewarded for this work by being given lambs of their own, and eventually, by the time they are in their late teens, they are assigned their own ear marks for their small flocks.

The boys and girls look forward to the summer, when school is out and they move out to the farming villages where their families maintain ranches. Although there is work for them in the fields and on the range there are also many activities that they cannot pursue in Zuni: hunting for small game, riding off in the hills, and swimming in the reservoirs.

During these years of growing up, the girls are trained to help their mothers while the boys learn to be farmers and stockmen. By the time the girls are ten years old, they are expected to help around the house in all sorts of ways: to clean the house, make the beds, wash dishes, carry out the trash, and keep the fire going in the stove. But the most important of their duties is to look after their young sisters and brothers, so that their mothers may carry on the household work without constant interruption. Among the more modern families a favorite chore is going down to the post office to get the mail or running an errand to the trading post.

In the earlier days the girls started to learn to make pottery when they were about fourteen years old. Today, with the disappearance of that art from most of the households, beadwork has become a substitute craft activity, and girls of a tender age may be seen seated around the table after the dishes have been cleared, cutting small bits of leather or sewing on beads--detailed, fussy work, which takes skill and infinite patience.

Children's games are many and varied. Some are familiar to children the world around: tag, hide-and-seek, stilt walking, tug-of-war, and rolling hoops. The girls play with dolls made of clay, baked in the ovens, or of cottonwood root, carved by the men. Boys and girls of ten years or less may be seen on any summer day swimming without clothes in the Zuni river. When they see a white man walk by there is a good deal of shouting and scrambling to hide from view, as they have learned that white adults disapprove of children going naked. Another favorite sport during the warm weather is racing on all fours with tin cans held in the hands. During the winter the children skate on the ice with skates improvized out of pieces of scrap metal.

As the children grow up, the play groups separate. The girls spend most of their hours with other girls, and the boys have their own groups. This occurs at about twelve years of age.

The boys have certain sports of their own: when they are about four years old, their fathers or grandfathers make them their first slingshots, these become progressively more lethal as the child grows older and his aim improves. Birds and prairie dogs are the favorite targets. Small boys practice kick-stick racing, a ritual type of racing in which, as men, they run a long course kicking a small stick. Now that these strenuous races (which used to be a favorite method of gambling) are dying out, young children take less interest in their own informal kick-stick races. The boys are also taught to make snares out of horsehair for catching small birds (the feathers from which are used for making prayer sticks) and dead-falls for catching rabbits and other small game, which are fed to the eagles caged in the village. These pursuits are especially favored by the boys when out on the sheep range, since they serve to break the monotony of long, lonesome days.

When the boys and girls are about six or seven years old they will occasionally indulge in sex play. The boys get on top of the girls and play at having sexual intercourse in imitation of their parents, whom they have probably observed in the close sleeping quarters. Or they may have learned of intercourse from watching the farm animals.

The principal method of disciplining the children is by scolding. If that is not effective or if the children grow callous to harsh tones, the parents may resort to scaring them. When they stray away from the house at night they are told that the witches will get them. If youngsters misbehave while playing in the house of an evening the mother may say: "If you aren't good you will have to sleep by yourself tonight," That threat quickly brings them into line. The children are also told animal stories to frighten them; there is a whole cycle of stories about the coyote and his tricks, and about the fearful and powerful bear who may carry them off if they are disobedient.

The most frightening of all threats for a child is to be told that Atoshle will visit the house. This scare Katchina has a horrible countenance, is dressed grotesquely in a large mask with a huge mouth, great protruding eyes, and disheveled hair and teeth, and carries a long sword in one hand and a cane in the other, while on its back is a basket in which naughty children are carried off. If a woman has a disobedient child she may request the kiva chief to send Atoshle to her house (Bunzel 1929-30b: 937-41). The children are told that this creature will eat them. Boys are also told that Atoshle will castrate them.

One informant, on being questioned about Atoshle, said:

> When I was about three my grandfather told me about Atoshle but my folks never had it at my house. They said that this dander [i.e. member of the Katchina cult] would come around if I did not behave and cut my balls off.

This bogey, according to the stories the Zuni parents tell their children, lives in a cave in one of the nearby mesas. If it sees the children stealing peaches in the orchards at the base of the mesa, it comes out and catches them and carries them off to its cave (Parsons 1939: 1, 50-52). Some of the braver children grow callous to these tales and say that there is no such a person, that the stories are told to make them obey. The situation was well described to Parsons by one of the older women:

> The woman was angry because the boy had mocked the katchina, and that was very dangerous, and she knew the boy would be punished. When the angry katchina did come to cut the boy's throat, his father raised his gun and threatened to shoot. Another katchina, Father Koyemshi, intervened and suggested that they merely cleanse the boy. "Don't cut off his head! Just cleanse him to frighten our friends. Whip him with yucca!" [Parsons 1939: 1, 52].

The whipping, it is said, does not take place. The Katchina is bought off by a bit of meat and other food so that he will neither whip nor devour the child. But the child's terror must be extreme, and at this tender age he learns two lessons: to obey his parents; and to have a healthy respect for Katchina.

While relatively few Zuni children have been visited by Atoshle (although every child has been threatened with such a visit), all of the male children continue to be initiated into the Katchina cult. The first phase of this ceremony may take place when the boy is only six to eight years of age. The ceremony used to be held in the spring of every fourth year. More recently the interval has been longer, with the result that some of the boys are well along in school before they pass through the first phase of the initiation.

For seven days before the climax of the ceremony, when the initiates are whipped in the plaza, the whole village is alive with preparations: the ceremonial fathers of the boys are notified of the approaching initiation by the child's parents; food is prepared for the gods and corn is ground by the women of the father's clan for the ceremonial father; the Katchinas enact ritually prescribed roles and utter long, letter-perfect prayers.

On the day of the initiation the ceremonial fathers escort their charges to the plaza, where they are whipped by the masked dancers. Each child receives seven lashes on the back from each of eleven masked dancers. But these lashes are not too painful--the boys are wrapped with padding. One young man tells of his initiation:

> Over me on his back he put several blankets
> and quilts and a wagon tarp on top of that.
> Then he walked slowly by the line of dancers
> and each one whipped me with the yucca. It
> didn't hurt at all. I had too much padding on
> me.

The boys are then taken down in one of the kivas, but first their sponsor stops at the top of the ladder for his novice to be disrobed. After a short time the boys and the sponsors reappear and additional whippings follow. This time there is less protective cover, and the child is in a kneeling position with his head between his ceremonial father's legs. Then, as told by one Zuni the following takes place:

> Now the Blue Horn comes. All around the plaza
> are the lines of boys, sometimes there are as
> many as three or four rows of them; the dancers
> come in, four of them, they feel the boys with their
> foot, if they hit you on the back square it hurts, so
> they feel you to find your rear end, . . . each one
> gives one blow, goes on to the next. They repeat
> that four times around, so each gets sixteen blows.
>
> Now the dancers get in line in the middle of the
> plaza. They take the coverings off you and put
> on only two blankets with the canvas covering;
> this time you are on the back of your guardian
> again. They all go through, pass the line of the
> dancers, each hits you four times now, this time
> you could feel the pain. Some boys cry for help;
> the people laugh.
>
> When all is through . . . the women, guardians,
> and boys go to one of the kivas, there are two kivas

> to go to. Then when you are in the kiva they
> come in and are seated, your guardian on one
> side, your sister on the other, and as they walk
> by praying they stop at each boy and give him
> the binan [breathe] through the mask. . . .
> You suck in. Then that is all.

For the following four nights the novice fasts, avoiding all animal food; on the morning of the fourth day the ceremonial father removes the boy's hair feather, the symbol of his novitiate, which was placed there during the initiation, and leads him to his house, where one of the women bathes his head in yucca suds, the symbolic purification that is the final act in so many pueblo ceremonies.

The final initiation takes place some years later. Many of the boys are only nine or ten years old, but some who have been away from the pueblo at school may be in their late teens before their final initiation. One man describes his initiation thus:

> My sponsor, the same man I had some years be-
> fore, came over to my house and took me over
> to _____'s house. There were seats and
> chairs all around the edge of the room. As it was
> my turn, my sponsor took me out toward the mid-
> dle of the room, and there were four Blue Horns
> there and two Mud Heads. The Mud Heads counted
> the lashes that the Blue Horns gave. I had my head
> between my sponsor's legs, who was standing up.
> My back was covered with only a single blanket
> and a buckskin. Each of the Blue Horns gave four
> lashes. It sure hurt this time and made me cry.
> My back was sore even the next day.
>
> Then in return I gave each of the Blue Horns a lash
> on each arm and leg. . . . Then after the whip-
> pings were over the Blue Horns took off their masks,
> and they put them on again and they were sprinkled
> with corn pollen by the sponsors. . . . The head
> of the Katchina society told us then that the
> Katchinas were not the actual gods but were being
> represented by human beings. He told us not to pass
> on these secrets to the small kids who had not been
> initiated. If we did, he said, the dancers would
> come and whip us without any clothes on.

Another man tells of the new status of the boy who has been through
the second degree of the initiation:

> Now you are allowed to see the masked dancers
> at night; if you want to take part in it your
> guardian comes over and gets you and takes you
> over to where the masked dancers are. You are
> allowed to dance with him [your guardian] in
> the masked dance. From there on you are on
> your own. You can dance whenever you feel like
> it.

Ruth Bunzel, the foremost student of Zuni ritual, compares this ceremony with our Christian baptism. She points out that the children are whipped
"to save them, to make them valuable." Before this they have no ceremonial status. If they should die they could not enter Koluwala·wa, "the house
of the gods." At the first of the two initiation rites the child, like the Christian child at baptism, is tentatively admitted to the congregation of the elect,
"until, having reached the age of understanding, he establishes his relations
with the supernatural by voluntary partaking of communion, just as the Zuni
child must, after reaching years of discretion, complete his initiation by being induced into the mysteries of the cult" (Bunzel 1929-30b: 976).

It should be pointed out that the whippings administered at this initiation and on other ritual occasions are not thought of as being punishment, but
rather as a mode of cleansing, a way of ridding the child of evil. Although
they are meant for purification, they are certainly as dreaded by the children
as if they were disciplinary.[47]

However, whippings in our sense of the word--to correct the behavior
of a child who is naughty--are not unknown in the Zuni household. One of
the older Zuni women said (Stewart 1940-41: August 1940):

> In the old days some Zunis really beat their chil-
> dren, made them black and blue. About one
> fourth of the Zunis would really beat their chil-
> dren. . . . The worse punishment would be
> hitting four or five times with a strap. Scolding
> and slapping was the next worse [punishment].

Whippings continue down to the present day. But there is little doubt
that the children are held in line more often by threats of the supernatural, by
scaring, and by scolding than they are by physical whippings. The main point
is that Zuni child training is not so permissive as it has been made out in the
anthropological literature. For example:

> The Zuni child, on the other hand, grows up under
> little restraint; he faces no stern disciplinarian in
> the house. Rather, his parents are all kindness to

> him and humor his wants. But where the Zuni mini-
> mize physical force as a sanction, they strongly
> emphasize shame [Goldman 1937: 339].

The first part of this quotation is an exaggeration, but credit is due Goldman for pointing out the importance of shaming in the educative process. It is quite possibly the most important single sanction in the upbringing of the Zuni child, and more than any other one factor shapes overt behavior in later life. The Zuni child at a young age is sensitized to ridicule. Being laughed at cuts him to the quick.

It is doubtful that the onlookers laughed when the Zuni boys were whipped, as mentioned above. But it is psychologically significant that the individual quoted associated pain with laughter. For the Zuni, being laughed at is pain. The sharpest rebuke from a parent is laughter, and this early con-ditioning develops a sense of shame which follows the individual through life. It becomes a problem in the classroom. One of the teachers tells of how the children will not come to school but will "play hookey" rather than appear in school with a pair of shoes of a slightly unusual style or a torn or unpressed dress. They are afraid of the jeers of the other children.

It takes years to get the children to speak out in the classroom, to overcome their shyness, and this hypersensitivity to shame is one of the reasons. In order to get results, it is often necessary to have the children work in groups of two or more, and some teachers even resort to having the children recite in teams. Otherwise the gibe of "big shot" is used by the others to shame the child who is thought too bold, too outstanding, too pushing. For this reason it is also more effective, the teachers have found, to ask the children to write their lessons rather than recite them, and even then the child may build a barricade of books around his paper so that no other child will know what he is doing.

This hypersensitivity to shame, of being more concerned with what the other person thinks of you than with what you "feel inside," as we would say, does not diminish during the course of life, but is kept sharp by other methods of social control: by gossip and by witchery. On his return to the pueblo, one of the veterans of World War II wore a business suit of a neat cut, with a thin pin-stripe, of which he was inordinately proud. When he went to the public shower, he carried his change of underclothes in a leather toilet case, rather than the usual brown paper bag. Word was soon passed around the pueblo, laughter was on all lips, and soon he conformed to the group and wore blue jeans and work shirt and carried a grocery sack.

So we find the genesis, in terms of the individual, of the "Apollonian" seeking of the middle road early in life as the child undergoes socialization within the home. He is cautioned of witches, of owls and coyotes that may be witches in disguise, and he dares not go too far away at night--even the adults are afraid to walk to the outskirts of the village alone in the dark. He is taught by his parents never to accept food from strangers. Why? Because it may be poisoned by a witch. And he learns from overhearing his family gossip which families they approve of and which families are "those jealous people," those who begrudge what little you have and who may work magic against you.

These attitudes and fears are best expressed by a Zuni woman, who in this instance is talking about her sister's family:

> Yesterday my niece [age 4] was playing outside her house. Her playmate asked her why her brother didn't join them. "Because he is sick," my niece replied. "Oh, maybe that old woman _____ witched him."

> She didn't know that old lady her playmate told her about. She came into my house and asked me what witching was.

> Other people say that maybe that old woman is a witch. She comes to visit at this house next door, but I don't tell my children she is a witch because they might say that in front of her and I don't want her to know that we are afraid of her. I am friendly to her and as long as I don't do anything to her she won't harm me.

> I would warn my children to keep away from her children and grandchildren.

This same woman speaks of another family:

> Another family is that way. Their son is in my boy's class at school. He is jealous of my boy and tells the teacher that my son does bad things which he does not do. I tell my son not to quarrel with him, even if he does say bad things, because he is of a witch family.

> That boy's younger brother is also mean. People say those boys are mean just so people will get after them. Then they will witch them. I tell my boy. . . . never to say anything to make them angry.

The mother does not show her anger toward the old woman whom she believes to be a threat to the lives of her niece and her children. For if she does display her anger this will antagonize the witch and cause her to work her spell. She passes on to her children that most important Zuni rule of conduct: never display your anger. Even if you are in the right, and fighting mad, do not show your emotion.

At this early age, when the child is still in the primary grades at school, his behavior toward his playmates is being shaped by the rules handed down by his elders. We find here the nascence of the overt behavior made famous as Apollonian by Ruth Benedict in Patterns of Culture. There she wrote:

> The ideal man in Zuni is a person of dignity and
> affability who has never tried to lead, and who
> has never called forth comment from his neigh-
> bours. Any conflict, even though all right is on
> his side, is held against him [Benedict 1934a:
> 99].

She also wrote:

> and he should without fail co-operate easily with
> others either in the field or in ritual, never be-
> traying a suspicion or arrogance or a strong emotion
> [Benedict 1934a: 99].

No one wants to anger the other person and suspicion is mutual; no doubt the old woman suspected of witchery is equally afraid of this woman who tells of the incident. Adults who appear to be so calm and who cooperate in village affairs do so out of fear of the other person, not out of trust.

Adolescence and Marriage

As the child gets on to adolescence, the Zuni parent of the present day has greater disciplinary problems, especially with the girls.

At Zuni there is no puberty ceremony for the girls, as there is in many North American Indian tribes. Even within the family no fuss is made over the girls on this occasion, they are neither excluded from society nor surrounded by taboo as are Indian girls elsewhere. In fact some mothers are so casual about the matter that their daughters are given little or no forewarning of what is to come. According to our informant:

> I started menstruating in the summer. I was twelve
> years old which seemed early. My sister _____
> started menstruating in the winter before me, although
> she was younger. My sister was at home, going to day
> school, I was at Black Rock. When I came home
> mother said _____ was bleeding and asked me if I
> had. I said no, but a few days later I did. I was scared,
> anyway. I was home and went to mother and asked her

what to do. I just wore a pad. My brothers and father
were told that I was an adult. I learned about menstruation by seeing older girls at day school undress, seeing
their pads around. We would ask girls if they cut themselves. Big girls told us to be quiet, that we would be
like that some day.

Premarital sex relations for girls before marriage is condemned, but,
as in many Western societies, there is a double standard of morality and the
boys are expected to have sexual experience before marriage. Frequently a
boy's first sexual experience is with an older woman, perhaps with a married
woman who has been divorced, simply because she is not carefully watched
by her parents.

In the old days courtship took place close to the girl's house, where
the mother could keep an eye on her daughter:

In the evening when I went for water X_____
would meet me and say he would meet me later.
Then I would go out with slop or for wood. X
would talk. My mother kept an eye on me. Then
one day my mother asked me to have him come in.
I gave him something to eat. He stayed all night.
First morning, he got up and went home without
breakfast, but left for all day. Each night he came
a bit earlier. About the third day he came for supper.

An older woman said:

If my daughter ran wild I would scold her, then I
would whip her. My daughters have all been good,
and I haven't had to whip them.

I would not say anything to a boy even if he had the
reputation of chasing. I told my sons not to steal or
lie, but never told them not to get girls before marriage.

This statement came from an old woman who was recalling the earlier
days of her youth. Today there is a good deal of premarital intercourse. The
close association of the boys and girls at school has made the problem of the
parents more difficult. Formerly the girls could be closely watched. Now that
is impossible. One of the Zuni women reports that in 1917: "there were seven
girls at the Day School who were pregnant." While this may be an unusually
large number, even at the present time there are likely to be several girls who
drop out of school during their high school days because of pregnancy.

One of the young Zuni men recalls his sexual adventures when he was
in high school:

After my dad found out what I was doing he did not
say anything to that girl or her folks. Zunis do not
do that. About a week after we started having intercourse I began sneaking into her house at night. She
used to sleep in a back room alone and she let me in
there. I used to go there about every night. Maybe
her folks knew it. I would sneak out early in the morning and then was sleepy in school all day.

The parents are very open in admitting that they have difficulty today with their daughters; there have been innovations at Zuni which have
complicated the problem of chaperoning the girls. During World War II the
Catholic mission began to show weekly movies in the recently constructed
gymnasium. The movies instantly became popular with the younger generation, who now did not have to go to Gallup to see a show. There was the
added attraction of being able to meet with the girls there, and in the words
of a Zuni parent:

Right after the shows, instead of girls and boys attending a show and going home directly, they will go to
some dark place, and those with cars take girls to the
mountains [mesas].

For this reason, plus the additional one that the children never wanted to miss
a show and the poor families considered this a drain on their supply of cash,
many of the older generation wished the governor and his council to take action and have the films discontinued.

The parent just quoted commented also on the change in village morals
since the old days:

After I got married and my sons grew up they [the
Zuni] still favored the old ways of living, but before they became grown the government set up the
school here in the village and that was the beginning
of the degeneration. After some people began to go
to school and speaking English then they began to
favor the white man's way of life. That was the first
indication of the changing ways. Although the people
carried on the old ceremonies they seemed to feel dif-
ferently towards them. And about the same time as
that the people began to drink.

Around 1927 conditions were a lot worse because all of
the children were receiving an education. So that was
the time the older people could hardly control the

younger people. The young people began to argue
with the governor and his officers. The children began to disobey their parents. Before that you did what
your daddy said, but now the younger people thought
that the older people were wrong.

So here at Zuni, as among the Navaho and the Sioux and most of the
ethnic groups in the larger North American society, there arises a conflict between the generations as the acculturation process progresses.

It was much easier for the elders to maintain control when Zuni families lived in extended-family units. But now there is a growing trend for
young married couples to set up their own households, independent of their
parents. The mother and father living in an isolated house have a more difficult time maintaining discipline than was the case when the siblings of the
mother and the grandparents were on hand to reinforce the parents. Control
by the parents has broken to the extent that at least one family, and probably
more, has requested the principal of the school to discipline their children.

The parents' problems in maintaining discipline may also be an indication that the traditional sanctions are not as strong as they used to be. It
may well be that the children are not as easily intimidated by the threat of
Atoshle as they were in former times. And it is not to be forgotten that the
strong arm of the society, as represented by the Bow Priests, no longer exists
as a disciplinary body for keeping the transgressor in line.

Perhaps the introduction of cars, more than any other factor, accounts
for the disciplinary problem of the parents with adolescent children. Now
that almost every family owns an automobile the problems of chaperonage
and drinking are serious ones for the parent of a Zuni adolescent, just as they
are for American parents, countrywide. The problem is even more complex
for the Indian community, where the child is undergoing not only rapid physical growth but also rapid change in his behavioral norms as he becomes acculturated to the greater society and estranged from the ways of his ancestors.

Eventually the young men and women settle down to thinking of marriage, and the traditional courtship pattern prevails, although modified in some
respects. There is the meeting of the girl and boy outside the house, and the
visits to the girl's house.

If a girl and boy decide to marry, he goes to her house and obtains the
permission of her father. If he is acceptable to her family the father gives his
daughter's suitor a short lecture along moral lines: that he must work hard and
be a good provider for his wife and children. Such a talk with the father ends
the period of courtship as far as the family of the girl is concerned and the son-
in-law is invited to share a bed with his wife. He accepts this offer with mod-
esty, even though he may have already enjoyed sexual relations with this very
girl in her own house. During the early years of the century, marriage was

accompanied by gift exchange: the man gave the girl a manta and the women of her household gave the women of his mother's house a basket of hand ground corn flour. Today even this simple exchange of property does not always take place, for mantas handwoven by the Hopi Indians are dear of price and hard to come by.

During the first days of marriage the new husband is bashful in the house of his in-laws and sneaks out each morning early. Finally he gains enough courage to remain at the bride's house for breakfast. The village recognizes the union as official when he appears in the yard and chops wood for his wife's family.

At Zuni the husband does not feel a part of the family until his wife bears a child, and divorce before this time is frequent. Today divorce is common even after the wife has given birth to several children and may be arranged by mutual consent. The children always remain with the mother, and her next husband assumes the role of father. The divorced male goes back to the household of his mother and sisters, where he lives until he re-marries.

Death Customs

Death is believed to be caused primarily by witchcraft, although death by accident is also accepted. Contagious disease is recognized as an immediate cause of death, but not the ultimate cause. The school boys and girls have learned of our germ theory and many know that measles, tuberculosis, and other diseases are caused by micro-organisms, but they have not completely given up their old beliefs and may simply say that the germs are planted in the individual by "those jealous ones." Even to this day the family of an individual who has contracted a lingering illness posts a watch on the roof of their home in order to detect the lurking witch.

At death the mother, sisters, and other female clan relatives of the deceased come to wash the corpse and prepare it for burial. Deceased males are dressed in white cotton shirts and trousers--the everyday dress of the male some fifty years ago and the ceremonial dress of the priests today. The corpse of a woman is garbed in a calico dress. Many hundreds of dollars worth of jewelry may be buried with the dead, for their spirits must be properly clad when they return to earth as Katchina dancers.

After a period of mourning, during which other members of the father's and mother's clan join the immediate family, sacred meal is sprinkled with the right hand and black meal with the left--the latter to ward off evil. The last to enter the house are the gravediggers, usually the father or brothers of the deceased. The corpse is sewn into a shroud of blankets, and the whole covered with a manta. The body is taken by a truck to the cemetery in front of the old Catholic church. There the grave is dug, for men on the south side of the graveyard and for women on the north. The head is placed at the east end of the grave so that the deceased, as he lies on his back, faces the Katchina Village to the west.

A tale is told of how witches steal the jewelry of the dead. They are said to dig a tunnel from a house adjoining the graveyard to the spot where the corpse is laid. Even young acculturated men and women insist that this practice goes on today. "How else," they ask, "can you account for the fact that no turquoise or jewelry is ever found when a new grave is dug, and only bones are exposed in the overcrowded churchyard?" The house of the tunneling witch is variously located, depending on who is telling the story.

Life on earth is not terminated by the death of the body. The souls of the dead will return each year in the form of the Katchina dancers and as clouds, purveyors of rain. "The dead form part of the great spiritual essence of the universe" (Bunzel 1929-30a: 483). Death is the life bringer[48] for the People of the Middle Place.

These, then, are some of the paths trod by the Zuni as they go through life. Our knowledge of them has come from the anthropological literature, from unpublished materials of anthropologists, from conversations with a number of people who know the Zuni well, and from personal experience. The remainder of the book has been derived from another source, namely from psychological tests applied to Zuni children. These tests could not supply the whole picture of Zuni culture, partly because children have not fully experienced it. They do, however, fill in one part of the cultural picture in greater detail than was previously known by providing data on how individual Zuni perceive some aspects of their culture and on the "raw material" of intellect, imagination, and emotion of which a Zuni is made.

PART II: A TESTING PROGRAM AT ZUNI

INTRODUCTION

The program of testing school children at Zuni was undertaken in 1942-43 as a part of the joint University of Chicago and Indian Office Project for Research in Indian Education. The school principal at Zuni, Mrs. Clara Gonzales, and two of the teachers, Mrs. Kathleen Erickson and Miss Marie Deatherage, attended the planning-training conferences in Santa Fe. These three people were chiefly responsible for carrying out the program at Zuni, although they were assisted in many ways by the entire teaching staff. In addition, Miss Josephine Howard of the Albuquerque Indian School teaching staff came to administer the Arthur test, Dr. Dorothea Leighton gave the Thematic Apperception and Rorschach tests, and Dr. Richard Birnbaum did the physical examinations.

This whole testing program at Zuni was greatly benefited by the fact that Mrs. Gonzales had been there as a teacher and principal for about twelve years and therefore knew the people well. It is notable that there was a very high percentage of success in getting responses from the children tested. Moreover, when she and the two other teachers went to interview the families of the children tested, she was well known to the parents and encountered less resistance than might have been the case for a stranger. Also she was able from her previous knowledge to verify or correct information supplied, and she could add considerably to what the families told her as to their economic status, place in the community, and such matters.

The materials that resulted from the research can be roughly divided into interview and background data, intelligence tests, health examinations, the psychological battery, and three projective tests. These categories can be more fully described as follows:

Interview and background material. Wherever possible, an English-speaking member of the family was chosen to do the interpreting for the interviewers, instead of an official interpreter. Older children in the family who had been pupils of Mrs. Gonzales and knew her well served in this capacity. The parents were questioned about the child's place in the family, his early training, what skills he had acquired, his health, and his relationships with his playmates and elders. The background material includes school records, data regarding the family from various government records, teachers' estimates of the child's ability and personality, and a few autobiographies written by some of the children at Mrs. Gonzales' behest.

Health examinations. Physical examinations of all school children are conducted every year by the hospital physician. For our convenience, in 1942-43 the doctor was willing to add certain procedures, such as blood pressure determinations, to his routine. In addition, previous health records were searched for what they could provide as to health history, immunizations, X-rays, etc.

Intelligence tests. These included the Grace Arthur Point Performance scale (Arthur 1933) and the Goodenough Draw-A-Man test (Goodenough 1926). Neither required the use of English, writing, arithmetic, or other skills learned only in school. With some of the smallest children an interpreter was used to explain what was desired. As mentioned before, the Arthur test was given by Miss Josephine Howard, while the Goodenough drawings were collected by Mrs. Gonzales or by the child's home room teacher. Of all the intelligence tests examined by the Committee, it was felt that these two were fairest as yardsticks of Indian child intelligence, because they appeared to be reasonably free of cultural bias.

The psychological battery. This was the name given to a collection of tests designed to sample the children's attitudes, sentiments, and moral and emotional reactions. They consisted either of questions and answers or of short stories followed by questions. Most of them were modifications of tests devised for European or American children by such psychologists as Piaget (1929), Bavelas (1942: 5, 371-77), and Stewart. With other Indian groups, these tests were given by the teachers and were entirely a matter of oral performance. This method was tried at Zuni also, but so many of the answers became "I don't know" that Mrs. Gonzales undertook to do all the battery tests herself. She found that she got much better results with many of the children if she let them write the answers to one question at a time rather than tell them to her. However, she always administered this individually, never as a group test, as was done with some white children.

The projective tests. These included the free drawings, the Thematic Apperception test (TAT), and the Rorschach test. Free drawings were collected from the Zuni children in most cases by the home room teacher. With the younger children, the whole class would participate, and only the drawings of those children selected for the study would be kept. With the older children, only the ones in the sample did the drawings. Pencils, paints, crayons, and various sizes of paper were available, and an effort was made not to direct the child in any way as to the subject matter he chose. However, Mrs. Gonzales found that with the older children there was a marked tendency for the girls to specialize in houses and designs for pottery and for the boys to restrict themselves to cowboys or to various Zuni ceremonial designs. She therefore insisted that they draw something different, although she did not specify what it should be. These older children appeared to feel a great need for privacy in their drawings. They worked on long tables in groups of five to ten, but they would use library books to build little walls around their working spaces. Thus it appeared that there was practically no mutual stimulation in respect to drawings.

Of the other two projective tests, the Rorschach was always given before the Thematic Apperception. The Rorschach test (Klopfer and Kelley 1942) consists of a series of ten standardized ink or paint blots, which have in themselves no meaning. They are shown to the child one after the other, and he is asked to tell what they look like to him, what he can see in them. This was always given as an individual test. Because of Mrs. Gonzales' experience with the battery, the older children were asked whether they would prefer to speak or write the answers. Several of them chose to write, but gave it up after the first few responses. In one case a child persisted in writing all his responses. From the things that a child sees and from the areas, colors, shading, etc. that he uses in forming his concept, it is possible to tell a great deal about his fundamental character structure and his habitual approach to life.

The Thematic Apperception test, as given to the Indian children, was a modification of the test devised by Murray (1943). A series of twelve pictures similar in subject matter to some of Murray's were prepared in simple line drawings by an Indian artist. These were presented to the child in series, and he was requested to tell a story about each one. Many of the older children at Zuni preferred to write their stories, and because of this it was possible to administer the test to several children at a time, passing the pictures from one to the other. However, the children showed no tendency to discuss the pictures or their stories with one another. Most of the younger children gave their stories orally. Very few pupils were tested who did not speak English, as Mrs. Gonzales felt that the presence of a third person as interpreter would seriously interfere with the child's performance.

Analysis of Tests

As with any group research, various parts of the process of collecting and analyzing this data were done by different people. This method has its good and bad aspects, making it possible on the one hand to encompass a much larger body of data than could be handled by an individual investigator (and also utilizing people with special skills at appropriate points), but on the other hand leading to certain discontinuities and occasionally to miscommunication.

As the data were assembled from all the Indian tribes in this study, they were sent to the Committee on Human Development at the University of Chicago. A few of the teachers and most of the professionals who had helped with the data collection also came to Chicago and took part in the analysis. For the rest, graduate students under the direction of Robert J. Havighurst carried out the painstaking and often tedious task of finding out what the tests could tell of Indian child personality. An effort was made to assign particular tests to those who had special interests or special pertinent background training. Thus, the medical records were assigned to the two physicians (Joseph and Leighton), who were also asked because of their training in psychiatry to analyze the Rorschach tests, along with Hassrick, and write up the test results for the tribal monographs. Since none of these people had had special work with Rorschach interpretation, they were sent to a training session under Bruno Klopfer and were encouraged to use him as consultant.

The Thematic Apperception tests were given to Henry to interpret. He had been at the original training conference for field workers as a psychological consultant and had participated in the design of the modifications of Murray's pictures. His method of analysis became his Ph.D. thesis and was later published (Henry 1947).

For the remainder, either the tests were analyzed according to established procedures (e.g. the Grace Arthur Point Performance test) or procedures were worked out by one or more graduate students under Havighurst's direction, with advice and criticism from the whole group of analysts and tribal experts who were involved in the research. Details of these procedures and test results on all the Indian groups and, in some cases, on white groups have been published in several journal articles (Havighurst and Hilkevitch 1944; Havighurst, Gunther, and Pratt 1946; Eubank 1945) and as a book (Havighurst and Neugarten 1955).

The present volume represents the last of a series of monographs in which an attempt was made to report the test results in a way that would enable the reader to consider the findings for each tribe against a description of the history and present cultural status of that tribe. This attempt led to almost insurmountable problems in some cases, for a writer had to be found for the tribal description as well as for the reporting of the research findings; and this compounded the difficulties of all research reporting by adding the need for collaboration between authors. However, except for this Zuni report, only a few years elapsed between data gathering and publication of the monographs.

Since at the time of this writing (1960) it is now eighteen years since the testing program began, one might well ask if the results have any meaning, or at least if they represent to any degree what one might find today if the same tests were repeated. Obviously one cannot state flatly that they either would or would not be the same without retesting. Undoubtedly there would be some alterations in content and imagery. Yet we feel quite confident that the fundamental outlines of Zuni personality as shown in the results of the tests reported herein would be seen in the same or similar tests given to a new generation of Zuni children within the next five to ten years. Very likely it would still be much the same even longer than that, for the Zuni change slowly even in the superficial expressions of their personalities. In any case, we deal here with aspects of personality which we believe do not change very much in any group, provided there is neither a large-scale intermixture with people of a very different sort of character structure and traditional approach to life nor a drastic and rapid cultural disintegration, such as took place with the Sioux (Macgregor 1946).

Selection of Subjects

At Zuni, all educational activities take place in the main village, and virtually all Zuni children from six years to about fourteen or sixteen attend school. It was therefore unnecessary to use more than one community to get a representative sample. There are four schools in the village--a government day school, a Catholic mission, a Christian Reformed mission, and a county public school. In the year of the testing program, the enrollment at the government day school was 270, at the Catholic mission school 193, at the Christian Reformed school 139, and at the public school none, a total of 602 Zuni children in school locally. An additional 23 children were in school elsewhere. The questioning of various Zuni, teachers, and missionaries led to the conclusion that there was no regular method for deciding to which school a child should go, although there may be some tendency for parents in the Catholic faction to send their children to the Catholic school. Some children attend all four schools in succession, others go to one and stay until they finish. If a child tries one school and does not like it or does not get along well, he may be transferred to another as an attempt at adjustment. The somewhat stricter insistence on regular attendance at the government day school makes it popular with some families and unpopular with others. Several families have had different children attending all four schools. Very few Zuni go to the public school, which is intended primarily for the children of traders, missionaries, and teachers. There seemed to be no particular advantage in selecting subjects on a numerical basis from the different schools, and since the teachers concerned in the study were all on the staff of the government day school, it was decided to draw the bulk of the subjects from that school. The school census list, which contained some 637 names, was used, and every seventeenth name was noted. This child and all his brothers and sisters between six and eighteen years of age were then taken as test subjects, including those who attended other schools. A list of 103 names resulted from this method, 51 boys and 52 girls. Ages were distributed as shown in Table III.

Table III

Age and Sex Distribution of Zuni Children Tested

	5-7	8-10	11-13	14-18	Total
Boys	6	12	12	21	51
Girls	10	14	15	13	52
Total	16	26	27	34	103

Although this is not a random sample in the strict meaning of the term, examination of the variation among individual subjects and of the range of economic and cultural positions of the various families indicates that it is reasonably representative of the tribe and might be considered adequate as a quota sample. It was altered in the direction of including fewer families than might have been the case with a strictly random selection, because of the limited time the teachers could give to family interviewing.

Although many of the children took all of the tests, for various reasons the numbers on which the test results are based were more limited than 103 cases. For example, the Arthur test is thought to be inadequate for use with children above fifteen years of age, while the Goodenough test is not a competent measure of intelligence beyond eleven years. As has been mentioned in connection with the Rorschach and Thematic Apperception tests, deficiency in English was a stumbling block with the younger children, for which reason some of them were not included. The numbers and sex distribution of the children whose tests were studied can be seen in Table IV.

Table IV

Age Range, Sex Distribution, and Total Number of Subjects for Various Tests

Test	Age Range	Boys	Girls	Total
Arthur	6-15	35	42	77
Goodenough	6-11	18	24	42
Psychological battery	8-18	44	40	84
Free drawings	6-18	46	45	91
TAT	7-18	45	37	82
Rorschach	7-18	45	37	82
Physical examination	6-18	48	49	97

CHAPTER 8

INTELLIGENCE OF ZUNI CHILDREN

Because it was found in testing Navaho children that experience with white culture and white schools had a good deal to do with the success of performance on the intelligence tests used in this study (Leighton and Kluckhohn 1947), it seems worthwhile to examine briefly the history of education at Zuni. An early anthropologist (Mrs. Stevenson) stated that the first school was established in 1879. Government records indicate, however, that the first school was a Presbyterian day school begun in 1882. Education has been continuous but by no means universal since that date.

The government established a day school in 1898 to replace the Presbyterian mission school, and there has been a government day school in Zuni ever since. In 1907, the government added a boarding school at Black Rock, which in 1928 was converted into a sanatorium for housing and teaching children who were below par physically or were suspected of tuberculosis. In addition to the government school, the Christian Reformed Church established a school in 1900 and the Roman Catholics established St. Anthony's Mission School in 1923.

Although the exact duration is not certain, schooling has been essentially compulsory for several years. Zuni parents have evidently found it to their children's advantage to acquire a few years of formal education. Zuni boys average about eight years in school, while girls spend seven or eight years. When girls marry and become pregnant they usually stop school, whereas the boys may continue even though married. About fifteen to eighteen students a year, at the time of this study, went to boarding schools at Albuquerque and Santa Fe for the upper grades and high school. They usually stayed about two years, and few actually graduated. It is recorded that one Zuni has graduated from college. The location of school-age Zuni children in the year of the study is shown in Table V.

Table V

School Enrollment of Zuni Children
6-18 Years Old, 1942-43

School	Boys	Girls	Total
Government day school	142	128	270
St. Anthony's mission	92	101	193
Christian Reformed mission	87	52	139
Total day school pupils	321	281	602
Boarding school			18
Sanatorium (for tuberculosis)			5
Married girls not in school			12
Total			637

From this account it can be seen that education at Zuni is long familiar and essentially universal. One would therefore expect that Zuni children would suffer less disadvantage in taking intelligence tests than was the case with Navaho children. Table VI demonstrates that this is so.

It is clear that the mean IQ earned by Zuni children on the Arthur test is not appreciably below that of white children. On the other hand, the Zuni children did considerably better on the Goodenough test than they did on the Arthur test. A group of white children who took the Goodenough test averaged an IQ of 101. 2, so that on this scale the Zuni surpassed the whites. It is worth noting also that even on the Arthur test, where the average IQ was slightly below that for white children, there is a higher percentage of the Zuni group on the superior and very superior levels than there is of the white standardization group.

A point of considerable interest which is not apparent on Table VI can be seen when the distribution of IQ's for all the five Indian groups tested is examined (Havighurst and Hilkevitch 1944). This is that the Zuni show a larger percentage falling within the "average" range than do any of the other Indian groups. In other words, there is less scatter among the Zuni children. Results of other tests also show this characteristic of the Zuni as compared with other Indians, which is congruent with the feeling anthropologists have always had regarding the Zuni tendency to conform to a group norm. However, conformity in intelligence levels is a rather different order of phenomenon from conformity in social behavior or in values and beliefs. It raises the question

Table VI

Distribution of IQ's Earned on the Arthur and Goodenough Tests

Level of intelligence	IQ	Arthur	Zuni Goodenough	White* Arthur
Very superior	140 and over		7%	
	135-139	3%	5	
	130-134	4	10	
	125-129	3	5	1%
	120-124	(10%	5 (32%)	2 (3%)
Superior	115-119	5	10	4
	110-114	7 (12%)	15 (25%)	6 (10)
Average	105-109	12	10	12
	100-104	13	10	15
	95-99	12	7	17
	90-94	17 (54%)	2 (29%)	17 (61%)
Dull-normal	85-89	10	2	12
	80-84	12 (22%)	(2%)	9 (21%)
Borderline	75-79		5	5
	70-74	3 (3%)	7 (12%)	(5%)
Mentally deficient	65-69	1		
	60-64			
	55-59			
	50-54	(1%)	(0%)	(0%)
Number of subjects		77 (6-15)	42 (6-11)	372 (6-15)
Median IQ		98.5		
Mean IQ		99.6	111.7	102.2

* Dr. Grace Arthur's standardization group

as to whether the rather marked tendency to conformity may arise in part
from some sort of genetic constitutional similarity resulting from centuries
of inbreeding.

Sex Differences

Table VII shows the difference in the average IQ earned by the Zuni
boys and girls on the Arthur and Goodenough tests and compares these averages
with the IQ's of white boys and girls on the Goodenough test.

Table VII

Sex Differences in IQ

| | Zuni | | White |
| | Arthur | Goodenough | Goodenough |
	Average IQ		Average IQ
Boys	99.6	122.1	98.3
Girls	100.0	104.0	103.4

Here one sees that the only significant difference correlated with sex is
the superior skill of Zuni boys in drawing a man, both as compared with Zuni
girls and with all whites. This masculine Indian superiority was also found in
both the other Pueblo groups tested (Havighurst, Gunther, and Pratt 1946). It
seems that it must be related to some difference in experience and training of
the Pueblo boys. Perhaps it is the training in acute observation of details in
ceremonial costuming and in preparation of ceremonial paraphernalia to which
the boys are exposed more intensively, at a younger age, and with much more
participation than the girls. The relationship of such training to the unfamiliar
Draw-A-Man test might be both superior manual skill and the habit of attention
to detail, meaning that the boys would tend to be more particular than the girls
about proportions and details, which lead to a higher score on this test.

CHAPTER 9

HEALTH OF ZUNI CHILDREN

While medical examinations of a group of school children can give some estimate of the state of health of individuals, they can by no means furnish a complete picture of health conditions in the group. They leave out of consideration entirely the epidemic diseases which for many generations have ravaged American Indians, and take no account of the numbers of children who should be in the group but who never reached school age. Vital statistics would help to fill in the picture if they were available. However, even in as compact a community as Zuni, where one would think it would be quite easy to assemble all the facts on health, birth, disease, and death, the records are far from satisfactory. To report such matters does not seem to interest the Zuni, and without their active cooperation it is difficult, if not impossible, to achieve accurate records. There is a belief held by some Zuni that to count living things will kill them, which adds to the difficulty of enumeration.

An attempt was made to get a picture of health at Zuni by questioning the doctor as to the main problems and the kinds of diseases that he had to treat. He listed as the most prevalent diseases: (1) scabies, impetigo, and other skin diseases (2) venereal disease, mainly gonorrhea (3) bacillary dysentery of infants and adults in the warm weather, and (4) tuberculosis.

He felt that the principal health problems of the Zuni were, in order of importance:

1. High infant and maternal mortality, due to a complete lack of understanding of the birth mechanism.

2. High infant mortality due to diarrheal diseases in summer. This problem he attributes to inadequate or complete lack of screening and little understanding of the part played by flies in spreading disease. A further contributing factor is the use of

the corral rather than a sanitary privy for excretory purposes.

3. Venereal disease. There is no understanding of prophylaxis of this disease, except possibly among those young men who were in the army. Germs as a cause of disease play little part in Zuni thinking (as of 1942-43). Moreover, the common practice of changing sexual partners rather rapidly contributes to the spread of this infection. Treatment is usually not sought until the disease is well established and the infection of others has taken place.

4. Tuberculosis. The prevalence of this disease is due at least in part to the lack of understanding of the means of infection, the spread of the disease, and its prevention. Undoubtedly, the general state of nutrition and the economic position of the Zuni also contribute their share, as do the somewhat crowded conditions under which the Zuni live.

Approximately 400 Zuni were treated annually in the hospitals as bed patients, another 450 at the hospital as out-patients, and an additional 400 at the nurse's clinic in the village. The doctor stated that the Zuni attitude toward the white man's medicine is one of reserved skepticism, except for a few converts who realize its usefulness. A large number of Zuni cling to their native methods of treatment. Teachers at the school have found that if they hear early in the morning that a pupil or a member of a pupil's family is ill and immediately suggest hospital care, this suggestion is often carried out; whereas if they wait until the Zuni medicine man has been called in, nothing short of the patient's death will stop the treatment he prescribes for four days.

One interesting feature of health at Zuni is the fact that these Indians seem to have developed an immunity to the eye disease, trachoma. Many of the old people have impaired vision due to this disease, but there has not been a new case at Zuni for many years, even though there has been no attempt at preventing the infection of others on the part of those with trachoma.

One factor that contributes to the large number of flies and, therefore, to the prevalence of dysentery is the presence in the village of numbers of animals, chiefly dogs and horses, with their accompanying wastes. These animals are kept right among the houses.

Although privies have been present in Zuni in small numbers for a long time, the great bulk of them were introduced about 1935. About half of these privies are kept padlocked, with each owner holding his own key. Possibly this is a necessary device to reserve the privy for the family who owns it and to keep it clean, but it certainly must encourage the use of the ground, particularly for children. Moreover, since privies are of relatively recent introduction, the older habit of not using them is still strong.

The findings of the hospital physician's annual examination of the school children on our list can be seen in Table VIII.

Table VIII

Percentages of the 97 Sample Children, Showing Various
Health Conditions by Group, Sex, and Age Level

Condition	Tribal	Boys	Girls	5-7 yrs.	8-10 yrs.	11-13 yrs.	14+ yrs.
Good health[a]	45%	48%	42%	13%	23%	54%	70%
Undernutrition[b]	20	19	20	27	31	19	6
Decayed teeth[c]	11	10	12	40	15	0	3
Enlarged tonsils[c]	23	21	24	40	31	19	10
Parasites[d]	40	23	54	100	61	31	0
Skin diseases[e]	3	4	2	13	4	0	0
Enlarged glands[c]	33	23	42	40	50	42	6
Tuberculosis[f]	4	4	4	7	0	0	10
Average height (inches)	54	54	46	51	57	62	
Average weight (pounds)	50	73	46	61	82	107	
Average blood pressure		99/59	99/61	96/58	97/62	100/58	103/60

a. "Good health" in this table means a robust physical state with no important defects. b. Undernutrition means an appearance of thinness, poor musculature, and lack of fat. c. The terms, decayed teeth, enlarged tonsils, and enlarged glands, are self-explanatory. d. Parasites are either body lice or scabies. e. Skin diseases are chiefly impetigo. f. The diagnosis of tuberculosis was recorded only after a child with suspicious signs had been X-rayed.

As with the other groups examined, it is quite evident here that the older children appear to be generally healthier than the younger ones.[49] The elimination of parasites among the older children is probably due in part to each child's taking the responsibility for his own cleanliness. Tuberculosis at Zuni seems to be of the two types familiar among white children, that of infants and of young adolescents.

It is of interest to note that for the boys and girls the average height is the same, but the average weight is 23 pounds greater for the girls. On the basis of appearance, one might expect such a difference between the weight of adult men and women, but the boys and girls do not seem to vary so much in body build. Adult Zuni men look rather lean and are taller than the women, while the women become stout at an early age and quite obese as they grow older. This difference is very likely related to the difference in their occupations, the men being much more active than the women. One can also speculate that it may be related to the female ownership of the food, once it is brought to the house (cf. p. 30), and to the matriarchal system, whereby the women are secure and the men have to depend for their food on either their own mothers and sisters or on the bounty of their wives.

Average blood pressures seem rather low by comparison with those in white records, even for the oldest group of children. One might therefore expect few cases at Zuni of disease associated with high blood pressure.

As far as can be determined from such physical examinations, the health of Zuni children seems to be fairly good. The percentage showing tuberculosis is about twice that for the white population generally, but the 7 per cent figure for the youngest age group we tested and 10 per cent for the 14 years-and-over group is approximately what is reported for a rural Minnesota survey of 1924 and is considerably less than reports of earlier periods for large cities. Since none of these studies was conducted like ours nor like each other, however, truly comparable figures are not available (Holt and McIntosh 1934).

CHAPTER 10

THE PSYCHOLOGICAL BATTERY

As was mentioned in the introduction to Part II, this battery consisted of a number of different tests. The results of four of these are included in this chapter, although more were given. The remaining tests did not prove useful enough to evaluate for all the groups tested.

One of the main problems with giving the battery and judging its results was the language difficulty. It is almost certain that with many of the Indian groups, where acquaintance with English was superficial, the finer shades of many of the questions asked were missed or misinterpreted by the children. Similarly, they doubtless used certain terms rather loosely in their answers which may have been misinterpreted by the evaluators. The language problem was less acute at Zuni than in many of the other groups, and success in getting the required number of responses per test was much higher, due in part to the excellent rapport of Mrs. Gonzales with the children and in part to the willing-ness of the children to submit to pressure. For example, if a child did not pro-vide three answers where three were required he could be told, "This is not enough; write some more," and he would do so. In some of the other tribes such a reaction is inconceivable: a request for more information would simply have met with a passive refusal.

The four sections reported here are as follows: (1) the Emotional Re-sponse test (2) the Moral Ideology test (3) a test of immanent justice and ani-mism and (4) a test of attitudes toward the rules of games. In addition to the information on reactions, ideals, and so forth, a good deal of data about as-sociated persons was acquired, which proved quite useful in differentiating the child's relations to his parents, siblings, agemates, and older and younger chil-dren.

The Emotional Response Test

This test was devised by Dr. Kilton Stewart (Stewart 1942) to find out what sort of situations or events children associated with feelings of happiness, sadness, fear, anger, and shame. It proved to be one of the most fruitful parts of the battery, due perhaps to the fact that it allowed the child considerable spontaneity in his answers. The child was asked: "Have you ever been happy (sad, afraid, angry, ashamed)?" He usually answered "yes" to this question and was then asked: "Please tell me a time when you were happy." This was repeated three times for each of the different emotions. In addition, he was asked: "What is the best thing that could happen to you?" and "What is the worst thing that could happen to you?" The average number of responses to each question for boys and for girls can be seen in Table IX.

Table IX

Average Number of Responses to the Emotional Response Test

	Number requested	Zuni		White	
		Boys	Girls	Boys	Girls
Emotion					
Happiness	3	3.2	3.3	2.7	3.2
Sadness	3	2.6	2.5	2.0	2.6
Fear	3	3.0	2.7	2.0	2.5
Anger	3	2.6	2.5	2.2	2.4
Shame	3	2.6	2.6	1.6	2.2
Best thing	1	1	1	1.1	1.1
Worst thing	1	1	1	0.7	1.0
Total	17	16.0	15.6	12.3	15.0
Number of subjects		44	40	159	209

The number of responses compared well with those of all other groups tested.[50] In a few instances they were exceeded in other tribes but in general they placed among the first. Outstanding at Zuni is the willingness of the children to give instances of times when they felt ashamed. The number of responses is considerably higher than for any of the other groups and may reflect as much as anything the confidence of the Zuni children in their examiner. [51]

In the following paragraphs and tables, percentages quoted were derived as follows: For each emotional reaction (happiness, sadness, etc.) the base is formed either by the total number of responses or the total number for boys/girls. All responses were scrutinized and grouped into categories, which were given names to characterize them. There were, however, quite a few responses to each section of this test which did not lend themselves to categorization with these larger groups and so had to be kept separate or grouped as "miscellaneous." These small groups are omitted from these pages, but would bring to a total of 100 per cent the various groups of percentages reported. The percentages, thus, are the number of responses in a given category divided by the total number of responses for the emotion. Since these tests are by no means precise mathematical measures, the percentages have been rounded off.

As examples of times when they were happy, the Zuni children produced responses which could be classified in the following categories: (1) amusements (which included such things as riding horses, playing games, and going to the movies), comprised 24 per cent of the responses (2) attending or taking part in tribal ceremonials, 15 per cent of the responses (3) receiving or possessing property, 13 per cent (4) travel, 11 per cent, and (5) family solidarity-- i. e. taking pleasure in being with or doing things for the family--8 per cent of the responses. This list by no means exhausts the variety of responses, but includes those showing the largest percentages. There is considerable difference in the proportion of responses allotted to these different categories by the boys and the girls, as can be seen in Table X.

Table X

Differences in Reaction of Zuni Boys and Girls
to the Emotional Response Test: Happiness

	Boys %	Girls %
Amusements	32	16
Receiving and possessing property	16	9
Tribal ceremonials	11	18
Travel	10	11
Family solidarity	5	11

The boys evidently derive more happiness from incidents classified as amusements and as receiving and possessing property than do the girls, while the girls rate higher than boys in their interest in tribal ceremonials and in family solidarity. These results may reflect the difference in position of Zuni males and females, with the boys leading the more active life, which is reflected in "amusements" and taking care of commercial affairs, while the girls are the more conservative pillars of society, as shown by their concern with religion and the family.

Responses dealing with times when the Zuni children felt sad could be grouped into the following categories: (1) sickness, accident, and injury-- 30 per cent (2) death, 23 per cent (3) loss of friends and family by sickness or by going away, also aloneness--11 per cent (4) aggression or wrongdoing by other people, 10 per cent (5) disappointment, 7 per cent, and (6) discipline or punishment, only 5 per cent. What slight differences there were between the responses of the boys and girls can be seen in Table XI.

Table XI

Differences in Reaction of Zuni Boys and Girls
to the Emotional Response Test: Sadness

	Boys %	Girls %
Sickness, accident, injury	40	21
Death	21	25
Aggression, wrongdoing by others*	9	12
Discipline or punishment	8	2
Disappointment	6	8
Loss of friends or family	5	16

*This category would undoubtedly include witchcraft, whether or not it was specified.

The most significant points of difference here seem to be the greater stress laid by the girls upon the loss of friends or family (a similar response to those regarding happiness), and the greater importance to the boys of sickness, accident, and injury, to which they are doubtless more prone than are the girls.

Responses dealing with times when the children felt afraid were categorized as follows: (1) objective dangers, which included dangers from animals, the elements, machines of various sorts, and such items as fear of the hospital and of the times when they were ill--44 per cent (2) fear of the supernatural, which included fear of animals associated with supernaturals--12 per cent

(3) aggression on the part of others, such as fighting and being chased--12 per cent (4) subjective danger, which included fear of the night, of mysterious things, and of being alone-- 8 per cent (5) discipline by parent or teacher, 6 per cent, and (6) delinquency, such as stealing, destruction of property, or school infractions--4 per cent. On this test, there was remarkably little difference between the responses of boys and girls, as can be seen from Table XII.

Table XII

Differences in Reactions of Zuni Boys and Girls
to the Emotional Response Test: Fear

	Boys %	Girls %
Objective danger	47	40
Supernaturals	13	10
Aggression by others	9	14
Subjective danger	9	6
Discipline	6	6
Delinquency	2	6

The slightly larger amount of concern on the part of the boys with objective danger probably reflects again their more active lives, which involve handling animals, being out in bad weather, and having to deal with automobiles and other machinery. The girls seem to be somewhat more timid about contacts with other people than the boys, as seen in the larger percentage of responses dealing with aggression by others. In view of the information contained in Part I of this volume, it seems likely that the two categories "fear of the supernatural" and "subjective danger" are really one, reflecting the pervasive awareness of and uneasiness about witchcraft and supernatural forces of all kinds (cf. p. 63f.). The percentages of responses in such a joint category would then be increased to 22 per cent for the boys and 16 per cent for the girls--20 per cent for the group as a whole.

Responses related to anger were categorized as follows: (1) aggression by others, 39 per cent (2) exertion of authority by others, 17 per cent (3) loss of property, 9 per cent (4) perversity or error on the part of animals, 9 per cent (5) inconsideration of others, 9 per cent (6) restriction in the attainment of desires, 5 per cent, and (7) personal inadequacy, 4 per cent. All but the last item seem to involve the misdoings of people other than the subject. Sex differences can be seen in Table XIII.

Table XIII

Differences in Reaction of Zuni Boys and Girls
to the Emotional Response Test: Anger

	Boys %	Girls %
Aggression by others	35	42
Perversity or error of animals	17	1
Exertion of authority by others	13	12
Inconsideration of others	11	6
Restriction in attainment of desires	6	4
Personal inadequacy	3	4
Loss of property	5	13

As previously noted it is likely that the large percentage of the boys' responses citing anger with animals reflects their frequent contacts with animals. In relation to anger as well as to fear, the girls seem to show a somewhat greater sensitivity to aggression by other people than do the boys. Having property taken from them angers the girls nearly as much as perversity on the part of animals angers the boys.

Experiences remembered by the children as causing shame were grouped as follows: (1) embarrassment in presence of others, 54 per cent (2) personal bad behavior and aggressiveness, 11 per cent (3) personal failure and inadequacy, 7 per cent (4) aggression by others, 7 per cent (5) poor appearance in public, 7 per cent, and (6) discipline, 3 per cent. The slight sex differences can be seen in Table XIV. The only difference of note is the greater responsibility felt by the boys for the behavior of others.

If we combine the categories that seem to belong together, we find that "embarrassment in the presence of others" plus "poor appearance in public" make up 61 per cent of the group's responses, while "personal bad behavior and aggressiveness" plus "personal failure and inadequacy" make up only 18 per cent. One might say that the larger of these two percentages represents what is commonly defined as "embarrassment," while the smaller represents "feelings of guilt." In the first case, other people are involved, while in the second case, other people are not necessary. If these two figures are compared with the corresponding figures for the white children tested, one finds that the white children have 12 per cent of their responses in the "embarrassment" category and 67 per cent in the "guilt" category. Based on these percentages, one might say that Zuni children are extremely sensitive to the opinion of others

Table XIV

Differences in Reaction of Zuni Boys and Girls
to the Emotional Response Test: Shame

	Boys %	Girls %
Embarrassment in presence of others	55	53
Personal bad behavior and aggressiveness	11	11
Aggression by others	11	3
Personal failure and inadequacy	9	6
Poor appearance in public	7	6
Discipline	2	4

and have comparatively little conscience, whereas the reverse is the case with white children. Among the various Indian groups tested, Navaho and Papago showed the same predominance of "embarrassment" over "guilt" as did the Zuni. On the other hand, responses of Sioux children and those at Zia reveal a pattern similar to that of white children, while the Hopi showed an approximately equal balance between "shame" and "guilt."

The chief categories of the responses to the question "What is the best thing that could happen to you?" fell as follows (1) possessing or receiving property, 40 per cent (2) meeting social expectations, that is, going to school, getting a good job, being industrious, or growing up--19 per cent (3) excitement and adventure, such as going someplace or playing a game--18 per cent (4) personal achievement, 7 per cent (5) personal pleasure or comfort, such as having plenty to eat or enjoying good health--4 per cent (6) family and group solidarity, 3 per cent. Differences between the boys and the girls can be seen in Table XV. The main differences are the higher ratings of personal achievement with the boys and of family and group solidarity with the girls.

When asked, "What is the worst thing that could happen to you?" the responses were grouped as follows: (1) discipline, 21 per cent (2) aggression of others, 13 per cent (3) bad behavior or aggression of self, such as stealing, fighting, being unkind, or general bad behavior--12 per cent (4) frightening experiences, both natural and supernatural--8 per cent (5) misfortune of the subject, such as going to or missing school, poverty, or losing something--8 per cent. The variations between the boys and girls can be seen in Table XVI.

Table XV

Differences in Reaction of Zuni Boys and Girls
to the Emotional Response Test: Best Thing

	Boys %	Girls %
Possessing and receiving property	37	42
Meeting social expectations	21	17
Excitement and adventure	18	18
Personal achievement	10	3
Personal pleasure and comfort	5	3
Family solidarity	0	5

Table XVI

Differences in Reaction of Zuni Boys and Girls
to the Emotional Response Test: Worst Thing

	Boys %	Girls %
Bad behavior or aggression on the part of the self	19	6
Discipline	15	27
Frightening experiences	9	7
Aggression of others	9	17
Misfortune of the subject	4	12

As usual, the girls dislike aggression of others more than the boys, and they are more sensitive, evidently, to discipline. Either they do not go in for as much bad behavior and aggression as the boys or else they do not feel as guilty about it. Finally, girls apparently suffer more misfortunes than boys at Zuni.

Themes of responses. If pertinent responses to each of the different emotions, as well as the "best" and "worst" thing, are put together, a rank order can be established for certain themes that run through all these responses. Presumably, this rank order indicates the type of concern that was "on top of the minds" of Zuni children in connection with their emotional reactions. Each heading includes whatever reaction there was on the subject covered in both a positive and negative sense. For example, under "achievement," both success and failure are included; under "property and possessions," both the gain and the loss. The details of the precise items included in each theme are found in Havighurst and Neugarten 1955. The rank order is as follows:

1. Embarrassment as a source of shame
2. Self-gratification
3. Aggression by others
4. Death of others
5. Fear of the supernatural
6. Discipline and exertion of authority by others
7. Property and possessions
8. Achievement

The responses grouped in this way were divided according to sex and according to age. They were also compared by tribal groups. The Zuni children won the distinction of showing the greatest concern with embarrassment as a source of shame of any of the groups. The boys were slightly more concerned than the girls with this, except at the age of 11-13 years, when the girls seemed to be acutely self-conscious. Boys showed a slight decrease with age for this category. Zuni and the other two pueblos, Hopi and Zia, were the three highest in concern over discipline and the exertion of authority by others. There was a slight increase with age in this concern at Zuni, and the boys showed slightly less of it than the girls, as has been seen in discussing the different emotions.

Zuni children mentioned the death of others more than any group except the Sioux and the whites. The boys showed slightly more concern with this topic than the girls, and there was no regular age trend. Sex differences in all these categories are so slight as to be of little statistical significance. The same might be said of age differences, except that where there is a regular downward or upward trend, the significance is increased. Thus, there was a slight regular increase in interest in achievement with age and a somewhat greater decrease in interest in self-gratification.

In the case of fear of the supernatural, the boys showed a slight increase and the girls a decrease with age. It is worth noting that this theme ranks only fifth of the eight themes, even though study of Zuni culture indicates that supernatural forces, both good and evil, are ever-present in Zuni thought. One wonders how these themes would rank if adults had been tested instead of children. The fact is that only in response to questions about fear was anything said that the test analysts felt could be classified as relating to the "supernatural." On the basis of everything we know of Zuni child-training patterns, it seems unlikely that these school-age children, particularly the older ones, were unaware of both aspects of Zuni beliefs. Thus one can speculate on two possibilities: either the need to keep these matters secret prevented the children from mentioning supernaturals freely or else the fact that the tests were given in school put the world of Zuni culture further from the children than if they had been tested at home. In connection with this latter suggestion, it is notable that at the Zuni school the pupils speak only English within the school walls and (essentially) only Zuni without. Or, again, supernaturals may be so taken for granted that, like breathing or eating, it is not necessary to mention them.

Other themes could doubtless have been selected, but this group was chosen because they seemed to show the most differences between the tribes and between the Indian groups and the white children. For contrast, the rank order of these themes for the white children was as follows:

1. Self-gratification
2. Death of others
3. Embarrassment as a source of shame
4. Property and possessions
5. Achievement
6. Aggression by others
7 Discipline and exertion of authority by others
8. Fear of the supernatural

The white children gave the highest number of answers of any of the groups dealing with the following categories: self-gratification (here they were closely followed by the Papago and Sioux), death of others, and achievement. In their interest in achievement they far outdistanced all the Indian groups. They rank much the lowest of any of the groups in their fear of the supernatural, which might be expected, and are also lowest of all in embarrassment as a source of shame and in aggression by others. They are next to the lowest in their concern with discipline and authority. One might expect that they would exceed all Indian groups in their interest in property and possessions, but this is not the case. For this theme, they are exceeded by the Navaho, the Zia, the Hopi, and the Sioux, while the Zuni show the least interest of any group.

In summary, one might say that there seems to be a rather striking contrast between the Zuni and the white children in that the Zuni children are preeminently concerned with the sort of appearance they make and in the relationship they have with other people, while the white children are comparatively free of this type of concern and more taken up with self and what self can do. It is by no means a question of either or, rather a matter of more and less.

Personal relationships. Let us now consider the numbers and kinds of persons involved in the answers to the Emotional Response test. It is worth pointing out that on this test there was no requirement for naming people, so that we have here spontaneous associations of various categories of people with emotional reactions, as contrasted to the more forced choice of praisers and blamers in the Moral Ideology test.

For the average number of persons mentioned per response, Zuni ranked with the other two pueblos among the highest three of all the groups tested. As was the case with practically all the other groups, at Zuni the girls mentioned persons a little more often than the boys. The rank order, starting with the emotion that evoked the highest number of mentions of persons, is as follows: (1) sadness (2) anger (3) shame (4) worst thing (5) best thing (6) fear, and (7) happiness. The sex difference noted earlier is most marked in connection with anger, best thing, and worst thing. In the case of the other emotions, there is comparatively little difference. This rank order differs from the rank order of other groups tested only in that anger heads the list in most cases, with sadness second. The sex difference, with the girls mentioning more persons than the boys, is common to all groups.

In order to summarize the findings so as to show the children's over-all emotional relationships to the people they mention, the items were grouped into two categories: "positive" emotions and "negative" emotions. The positive emotions included responses to happiness and best thing, while the negative included fear, anger, and shame. Worst thing and sadness were omitted entirely, as being neither clearly negative nor positive, this decision being based on a study of the responses. Table XVII shows the categories of persons involved in the positive and the negative emotions.

Table XVII

Persons Involved in "Positive" and "Negative" Relationships to Zuni Children

Category of persons	"Positive" emotions			"Negative" emotions		
	Boys %	Girls %	Average %	Boys %	Girls %	Average %
Family	7	14	11	7	6	6
Father	34	19	26	5	0	2
Mother	5	12	8	5	8	6
Sibs, same sex	7	0	4	3	7	5
Sibs, opposite sex	0	6	3	3	3	3
Total family	53	51	52	23	24	23
Agemates	17	17	17	29	33	31
School, teacher	0	6	3	3	6	5
"They," somebody	12	14	13	25	26	25
Supernatural	0	8	4	3	2	3
Miscellaneous	18	4	11	17	9	14
Number of mentions	42	51	93	183	173	356

The figures of Table XVII show (1) that persons are more often associated with negative than with positive emotions, and (2) that individuals in some relationships are considerably more important than others in the emotional experiences of the Zuni children. There are, moreover, some striking differences between the individuals mentioned in connection with positive and negative emotions. For example, the father rates high in a positive sense, and low in a negative sense. For the positive emotions, the rank order, not including the miscellaneous category, is: (1) father (2) agemates (3) "They" or somebody (4) family in general, and (5) mother. It is notable that the father seems more important to the boys than the girls, while the mother and the family in general are more important to the girls than to the boys. However, the father is considerably more important to both sexes than is the mother. This seems a bit incongruous in a mother-centered society. Is it, perhaps, not quite so strongly mother-centered in practice as in theory? Or does the mother represent to the child the social pressures of Zuni culture to such an extent that their relationship is more formal than warm? In this latter circumstance, the father might well appear as a much less formalized relative, with whom the child can establish a freer and warmer association. Still another possibility is that in the matrilineal family group often there are several females, such as the grandmother and maternal aunts, who share the mother role to the child in many respects. This fact might well dilute the mother-child relationship, whereas in this same group the father is something of an outsider and doubtless stands out more as an individual to the child than do other family members. It is noteworthy that there is no great negative emotional response to the mother, just a comparatively small positive response. Perhaps all that can be said with certainty is that, whatever else her spheres of importance, the mother figures less in the emotional life of the child than does the father.

In connection with the negative emotions, agemates rank highest, "they" or somebody next, and then, after a marked drop, come siblings of both sexes. Fourth place is shared by the family and the mother, and school and teacher come fifth.

To measure the relative importance of family members versus outsiders, one can add up the percentages of the first five items on the table for family members and of the next three items for nonfamily members. In the case of the positive emotions, 52 per cent of the persons mentioned are members of the family, whereas 33 per cent are outsiders. For the negative emotions, only 22 per cent are family members, while 61 per cent are outsiders. From this it would seem that the members of the family, particularly the father, represent to the child a source of happiness and security, while outsiders remain largely a threat. At the same time, the comparatively high rank held by agemates and by "they" or somebody in both the positive and negative emotions is suggestive confirmation of the large part played by extrafamilial social pressure in Zuni child training--a further reflection of the fact that Zuni is a "shame" culture rather than a "guilt" culture.

Bavelas Moral Ideology Test

In contrast to the Emotional Response test, the Moral Ideology test was devised to give examples of the official moral values of the group studied, rather than private experience. The child was asked: "What could a boy/girl of your age do that would be a good/bad thing to do so that someone would praise/blame him/her or be pleased/think badly of him/her? In connection with the "good things," a second question was asked: "Who would praise him/ her or be pleased?" In connection with the "bad thing," the second question was: "Who would blame him or think badly of him?" An effort was made to obtain three examples of good things and three of bad things, along with a praiser or blamer, respectively, of each. As with the Emotional Response test, at Zuni the responses to the Moral Ideology test were in most cases written rather than oral. The tests of 44 boys and 44 girls were studied. The average number of behavior responses per subject was 6.0 and the average number of surrogate responses (praisers and blamers) was 5.8.

In analyzing the responses to this test, both for the Indian and for the white groups, it was found to be a common practice for children to mention two or three things that were good to do and their opposites that were bad, e.g. good: to help my mother; bad, not to help my mother. This raised serious problems as to how to categorize the responses. Finally it was decided not to try to distinguish between good and bad behavior, but to limit the analysis to finding out how often various types of behavior were mentioned and how they could be grouped into categories. The persons cited as praisers and blamers could be analyzed, of course, in much the same way as the persons associated with positive and negative emotions in the Emotional Response test.

After a number of experiments, it was decided to use the total number of responses as the basis for the percentage rather than the number of children giving responses. Furthermore, in some instances a type of behavior was placed in more than one category in order to measure its importance in relation to other things. For example, "doing work for my father" would be classified under the heading Work and also under Family solidarity and family work; whereas "Work hard" would be found only under Work. Thus the percentages shown in Table XVIII cannot be mutually exclusive, but indicate, rather, the proportion of the total responses that fell into various categories, some of which include others on the list. The white group is given for comparison, since most readers will have greatest familiarity with white children. The very interesting comparison between tribes will be found in Havighurst and Neugarten 1955.

Table XVIII

Categories of Moral Ideology Responses
of Zuni and White Children

Category	Zuni			White		
	Boys %	Girls %	Average %	Boys %	Girls %	Average %
Amusements	5	1	2	8	3	6
Work	50	42	46	11	9	10
Aggression	11	10	11	3	2	3
Stealing	12	5	8	2	2	2
Drinking	2	0	1	2	2	2
Bad language	0	0	0	2	2	2
Care of property	3	6	5	4	3	4
Thoughtfulness and kindness	2	15	8	9	13	11
Family solidarity and family work	41	48	44	13	15	14
School	4	5	5	9	12	10
Religious observance	0	0	0	2	3	2
Sexual morality	0	5	3	1	1	1
Witchcraft and evil thought	0	0	0	-	-	-
Total Responses	266	240	506	5333	7105	12,488

Table XVIII raises a number of interesting points. In the first place, one can see that work plays by far the largest part in the moral values of the Zuni children. One suspects from the figures that the two categories, "work" and "family solidarity and family work" mean nearly the same thing. This is not surprising since most children within the age range of eight to eighteen years live at home and do most of their work around home. The category containing the third largest number of responses is aggression, which is similar to what was found in the Emotional Response test for the Zuni children. Stealing, the next highest, might well be thought of as aggressive behavior, too. The fifth most numerous category, thoughtfulness and kindness, seems to be almost entirely a female concept.

It is interesting that no mention is made of religious observances at Zuni, in spite of the large part played by such activities in the lives of children from the youngest age up. Similarly, although witchcraft is reputed to be an important force there, it was never mentioned. It seems probable that the religious observance is too much taken for granted to require mention, which may also be the case with witchcraft. Further, it seems unlikely that witchcraft would be suggested as even a "bad thing to do" by a child in the context of this test--witchcraft is what some grownups do, not children. Other points of contrast between the sexes are: the greater attention of boys to work in general, to stealing, and to drinking; and the greater attention of the girls to care of property, to family solidarity and family work, and to sexual morality.

By contrast with the percentages of the Zuni responses in the various categories, there is no clear preponderance of any one category over the others among the responses of the white children, but rather a general scatter from the top to the bottom of the list. The five highest numbers in rank order are: (1) family solidarity and family work (2) thoughtfulness and kindness (3) school (4) work, and (5) amusements. The scatter may indicate the comparative cultural diversity in regard to Moral Idology among white children even in a group from as small and supposedly as uniform an area as this group of children represents. In other words, Zuni morality is social rather than individual; Zuni moral values are much more uniformly held than are white moral values. It probably reflects also the greater heterogeneity and complexity of white American culture anywhere as compared to Zuni culture. There is much less difference between the sexes among the white children. As with the Zunis, the white girls show somewhat more concern than the boys with thoughtfulness and kindness and with family solidarity and family work. There is equal concern on the part of both sexes with sexual morality.

One might expect to derive from a study of the surrogates, that is, the praisers or blamers of the good or bad act, the same type of information as came from the study of the persons involved in the Emotional Response test. Although the number of surrogates is so small in some cases as to be not very reliable from a statistical point of view, still some of the differences are so striking that they seem to be significant. Table XIX shows the parts played by the various types of individuals mentioned as "praisers" and "blamers" for both the boys and the girls.

These figures confirm that the category including members of the family is by far the most important. Of the family members, the father and mother play the largest parts, the father for the boys and the mother for the girls. The roles of the two parents as "praiser" or "blamer" are approximately equal. While family members provide the largest number of surrogates for all groups tested, the Zuni stand among the two highest groups in the total percentage

Table XIX

Praisers and Blamers Mentioned by Zuni and White Children

	Zuni				White	
	Boys		Girls		Both sexes	
	Praisers	Blamers	Praisers	Blamers	Praisers	Blamers
	%	%	%	%	%	%
Family	79	75	78	66	47	43
Father	36	39	8	11	7	3
Mother	20	16	42	45	15	15
Grandparent	6	2	3	4		
Elders	2	3	0	2	1	2
Agemates	4	1	6	1		
Teacher	7	5	14	17	14	18
Everybody	1	5	2	0	12	15
Government	2	0	0	0	5	3
Self	2	0	0	1	3	3
Recipient of the act	3	9	0	2	4	4
Total surrogates	131	128	120	112	5723	8617

* Family here includes parents and grandparents as well as any mention of
"family" as a whole or various other family members.

of mentions in this category. Evidently it is at home that the Zuni child receives most of his moral training and gets the most praise or blame for adherence to or lapses from the Zuni moral standards. Apparently the mother plays
a somewhat larger part with the boys than does the father with the girls. It is
to be expected that the parent of the same sex would be the most important to
a child from the fact that the father does most of the training of the boy in his
agricultural work, while the mother teaches the girl her role as housewife. It
is surprising that the grandparents are so seldom mentioned, considering that a
grandparent is very often a member of the Zuni household. It is possible that
the mother and grandmother are not distinguished as surrogates, and that the
same is true for father and grandfather, as was suggested in the discussion of
persons mentioned in connection with the Emotional Response test (see p. 106).

A comparison of Table XIX with Table XVII (persons involved in the emotional responses) shows clearly that the family members and people outside the family play somewhat different roles in the life of Zuni children. Thus, outsiders are comparatively unimportant in relation to moral ideology, whereas they have more to do with the emotional reactions of the children.

By comparison, the responses of the white children show that the family is of less significance in moral training than is the case with the Zuni children. Moreover, the father is less important for both sexes than even the teacher or "everybody." Outsiders of various types play a much larger role with the white children: mother, teacher, and "everybody" are about equal. The emergence of conscience is seen to a slight extent in the part played by self as a surrogate of the goodness or badness of an act (Havighurst and Neugarten 1955).

Immanent Justice and Animism

The test used here to determine the extent of the Indian children's belief in immanent justice and animism is a modification of the story used by Piaget (1929: 250 ff.). The following story was told:

> This is a story about two boys. These two boys, named Jack and Paul, were out walking and they came to a melon field. Each of them stole a melon and ran off to eat it. But the owner of the field saw them and ran after them. He caught Jack and punished him, but Paul got away. The same afternoon Paul was chopping some wood and the axe slipped and cut his foot.

Following this story the children were asked these questions.

A. Why do you think Paul's foot was cut?
B. If Paul did not steal the melon, would he cut his foot?
C. Did the axe know that he stole the melon?
D. Do these things happen only in stories or do they really happen?

The first two questions were designed to determine whether the children felt that a wrong act brought its own punishment, while the third was designed to see whether or not they viewed the inanimate axe as a living thing. The fourth question was asked to evaluate their attitude toward the story as a whole, but as such it was a failure and was not scored. The results of all the questions were less clear-cut than had been expected, partly perhaps because of language difficulty. Whereas Question A is quite straightforward, all the others require a considerably more extensive familiarity with English than was the case with the foregoing tests, and the formulation of the answer was also more complicated. Had this test been given in the Zuni language, it is possible that the results would have been more definitive.

White children tested by Piaget, by Lerner, and by others, have indicated that belief in immanent justice is highest in the younger children and that it decreases quite markedly with age. The Zuni children, by contrast, showed only a slight decrease in the number who believed in immanent justice from the youngest to the older age groups. The percentage for the children from 6 to 11 was 60 per cent believing in animism, while for those from 12 to 18, it fell to 52 per cent. Not enough children took this test to quote a year-by-year change. In only five of the other twelve Indian communities tested were the changes with age of statistical significance, but in all of these, like Zuni, the trend was in the same direction as that expected, based on the results with white children. That is, the youngest children showed the greatest belief in the immanent justice and animism of objects and the oldest children showed the least.

Attitude of Zuni Children Toward Rules of Games

This test was undertaken to get some measure of the balance between adherence to moral rules imposed by outside agencies and those due to an autonomous morality. Piaget found that what children said about the rules of a game corresponded quite closely to their behavior in the game itself and showed rather consistent changes with age. Thus, young children tended to believe that rules were unchangeable, whereas older children took more responsibility for the rules themselves and felt that they could be changed by common agreement.

The test was given by first discussing with the child some game that he knew. At Zuni the great majority of children chose baseball, football, basketball, or dodgeball. Then the following questions were asked of the child:

1. Do you know a rule in this game?
2. What do you think? Who made this rule first?
3. Can boys or girls like you make new rules?
4. Can small children make new rules?
5. Can bigger boys and girls make new rules?
6. Can rules be changed?
7. If the answer to 6 was "yes," How can rules be changed?
8. If the answer to 6 was "yes," By whom?

In response to Question 2, 35 per cent of the Zuni children attributed the rules to teacher, coach, referee, or athletic association; 11 per cent attributed them to white people; 8 per cent to players, boys and girls; 4 per cent to big boys and girls. Of the number who said "yes" to Question 6, the following groups of people were given as answers to Question 8: 12 per cent said that big boys and girls could change the rules; 9 per cent thought that teacher, coach, referee, or athletic association could do so; and 7 per cent said that players, boys and girls, or anybody could change the rules.

Table XX shows the percentages of children who believed that rules could be changed, and by whom they thought they could be changed. In other words, the positive answers to Questions 2, 3, 5, and 6.

Table XX

Attitudes Toward Rules of Games, by Age and Sex
of Rules Changers

Age	Sex	Younger children	Same age	Older children	Can be changed
		(Q. 2)	(Q. 3)	(Q. 5)	(Q. 6)
		%	%	%	%
5-7	Boys	0	0	20	40
	Girls	50	17	0	17
8-10	Boys	0	25	43	43
	Girls	0	36	64	54
11-13	Boys	0	8	67	67
	Girls	13	53	67	38
14-18	Boys	25	45	75	35
	Girls	25	63	75	50

For all but the youngest children, the least latitude in changing rules is accorded to children younger than the subject, the second largest amount to children of the same age, and the greatest amount to older children. There appears to be an increasing belief with age that rules can be changed until one reaches the oldest age group, when the number who believe that rules can be changed is less than in the preceding group. In most cases, the girls seem to have less conviction of the fixity of rules than the boys. However, it is everywhere apparent that responses to Question 6 are not necessarily congruent with responses to Questions 2, 3, and 5. The children may have felt that they had given the wrong answers before when they were asked Question 6, or may have been confused by so many questions that were so nearly alike.

The results of this test were compared for each of the six Indian groups, to see which showed the highest degree of constraint by outside rules and which showed the least. A composite rating for each tribe was arrived at by adding up the rank number of that tribe on each of the questions shown in Table XX. While this cannot be taken as a highly accurate indicator, it is interesting to see the results. It appears that the Zuni children showed the highest degree of outside constraint of all the Indian groups. Next come the Papago, the Sioux, Zia, Hopi, and finally the Navaho. From this, it appears that at Zuni there is more tendency to adhere to externally imposed or traditional rules and less to develop an autonomous or individualistic morality than with any of the other groups. The polar positions of Navaho and Zuni in regard to this quality agree well with anthropological descriptions of the two tribes.

CHAPTER 11

THE PROJECTIVE TESTS

As mentioned in the introduction to Part II, the projective tests included the free drawings, the Thematic Apperception test, and the Rorschach test.

Free Drawings

The method of collecting these drawings has been described (see page 82). Zuni has a very nearly perfect record for producing the desired eight drawings per child. The drawings were never completely analyzed from the psychological point of view, but what was done with them will now be described.

In the first place, many of the Zuni drawings, particularly those of the older children, are excellent from both the technical and the artistic points of view. Those of the younger children are naturally somewhat cruder. Readers who associate Indian paintings only with representations of ceremonial dancing figures will be surprised to learn that none of these were drawn by the Zuni children. To be sure, the boys drew a certain number of ceremonial designs, but they were limited to the type of design that is used on the ceremonial equipment--mostly intricate, brightly colored geometric symbols.

The analysis of the drawings consisted principally of counting and classifying the various things drawn and studying them qualitatively to see what they revealed. The Zuni children drew an average of 5. 3 different items per picture, which gave them fourth rank among the six Indian groups studied. Thirty-six per cent of these items could be classified as landscape, 11 per cent as animals, 10 per cent as humans, 16 per cent as dwellings, 15 per cent as other structures, 4 per cent as transportation, 2 per cent as schools, 3 per cent as crafts, and 3 per cent as ceremonial objects. The principal age and sex differences were that the younger children drew more humans than the older children, whereas craft and ceremonial objects were almost entirely limited to the two older age groups. Boys drew many more animals than girls, girls drew many more houses than boys. Only girls drew craft designs, and only boys ceremonial designs.

By dividing the items drawn into those pointing toward acculturation to white culture and those which indicated adherence to native ways, certain conclusions could be reached regarding the influence of white culture on the Zuni children. Landscape and items like cattle and wagons, which were introduced long ago, were considered "neutral" in this respect. The percentages of items that could be classified as native or as coming from white culture can be seen in Table XXI, grouped according to age and sex, and also averaged for the whole group.

Table XXI

Items in Free Drawings Showing Relative Influence
of White and Native Cultures

	White culture %	Zuni culture %	"Neutral" %
5-7 years	34	41	25
8-10 years	27	27	46
11-13 years	21	27	52
14-18 years	13	34	53
Boys	24	26	50
Girls	25	32	43
Average	25	30	45

From this table it seems apparent that the oldest group of children and the youngest are the most conservative, judging from the proportion of items showing Zuni cultural traits. The boys show a nearly even balance between white and Zuni cultural influences, while the girls mirror Zuni culture to a greater degree. The average for the group as a whole is also on the conservative side, although there is less difference in the percentage of items representing each culture than one might expect from descriptions of Zuni. Zuni figures are contrasted in this same way with those for the other six Indian groups in Table XXII (Mordy n. d.).

Table XXII

Percentage of Items Showing White or Native Culture for the Six Indian Groups

	White culture %	Native culture %	Balance in favor of native culture %
Zia	20	42	+22
Hopi	19	33	+14
Zuni	25	30	+ 5
Navaho	23	27	+ 4
Papago	33	16	-17
Sioux	41	15	-26

It is interesting that the three Pueblo groups appear to be the most con-servative and that the Navahos follow after them, with the Papago and the Sioux both showing strong evidence of white cultural influences. It appears that the free drawing test gives a fairly reliable indication of the state of preserva-tion of the aboriginal material culture, for certainly the culture of the Pueblos and the Navaho has been better preserved to date than that of the Papago and the Sioux.

Thematic Apperception Test

While the Thematic Apperception test has been used largely as a means of individual diagnosis, it is possible to learn a good deal about the general pat-tern of life and social interaction of the group by studying the tests from groups as homogeneous as those of the various Indian children. It is this aspect of the test that will be discussed here, while its interpretive value in regard to individ-uals will be seen when individual Zuni children are considered. The following impressions, provided by William E. Henry, give an interesting parallel to the findings of the intelligence tests and the psychological battery (Henry 1947).

The stories that the children wrote indicate that the economy of Zuni is primarily one of agriculture (corn) with some sheep, although there does not exist any marked anxiety about the crop or about food in general. It would ap-pear that while rain is sufficiently vital to have a prominent place in the religi-ous ritual, earning a living from the soil has not been too difficult. There is more evidence of acculturation at Zuni than at Hopi, but it has been accomplished without a great deal of conflict. The Zuni have incorporated into their daily life desirable aspects of white culture without allowing it to challenge their own cultural facts and traditions, and without giving up their unity and cohesiveness as a culture.

Group pressures and demands are the principal means of control over individual behavior. These social controls are directed toward removing signs of individual achievement or variation and toward the maintenance of the group character. The children are well aware of the power of these controls and recognize clearly that one must act in such a way as to fulfill the group demands and deny any personal desires for distinction. This trend toward the social norm extends into all spheres of life and prohibits excesses of a personal or social nature.

As a social group, the Zuni seem to be far more unitary and single in their aims and purposes than the other Indian groups studied. There exists great social cohesion and a smoothness, even a sophistication, of functioning that is outstanding when compared to the internal bickerings of the Hopi (Thompson and Josephs 1944) or the disorganization and looseness of the Sioux (Macgregor 1946).

Such group pressures as these necessitate a repression of individual spontaneity that might be expected to engender dissatisfaction and a need for the release of aggression. While this repression is distinctly present, and while there would seem to be also an undercurrent of tension and potential revolt, the adjustment that these people have made seems to have greatly reduced the anxiety and hostility, namely by social controls against its expression and by the other means described below.

The ceremonial life of Zuni is rich and fulfilling. This life is well systematized and well integrated into the daily living of the people. The children seem to have a great feeling for its importance and vitality. In this ceremonial life, the man has the major role, a role which is valued by the community and recognized by all as important and necessary.

The family is clearly organized around the mother, and the father takes a subsidiary position. However, the father has a clearly recognized place and is an integral part of the family life. Some of his prestige may come from his role in the ceremonial life. The mother is recognized as the authority and main disciplinarian, although the father also has a disciplinary function. There is little systematic hostility toward the mother. Adult authority is recognized, and obedience is expected but not compulsory. The children have, in general, not very much antagonism to adults and not as much covert aggression as the children of Hopi showed toward their parents.

Interpersonal relations are genuinely friendly. While the concept of roles and the behavior appropriate to them exists and is followed, within this limiting framework interpersonal behavior is related to personal emotions and feelings, and the need to behave in an appropriate fashion has not destroyed spontaneity in feelings. The stories indicate that gossip and bickering as a means of social control and stealing and petty aggression as a means of reducing tensions are present, but these seem to be of minor importance and of less vitality than the respect for other individuals and the recognition of personal motivation.

The main feature of the personality of the Zuni child is clearly an emphasis on conscious control aimed at the maintenance of smooth outer functioning without wide variations or personal excesses. However, this exists without the accompanying deadening of the inner life which has been seen in other groups. The Zunis' use of imagination has forestalled this deadening, and has contributed toward the relative smoothness of their overt social behavior.

While this constrictive and smooth outward functioning is the most outstanding aspect of the Zuni personality, it is only one part of the picture. The anxiety upon which such an adjustment is based and the need for aggressive release engendered by such inhibitions represent the other part. These tendencies seem to be well handled in Zuni both by the social sanctions against the expression of aggression and by a rich and well-integrated system of sublimation. The major aspects of the sublimation system would seem to be: (1) the rich and systematized ceremonial life (2) arts and crafts,and (3) the great concern with practical realities and with details. While the type of concern shown for details is in a sense "compulsive," it is one of the Zunis' major defense mechanisms in that it drains off attention and energy, which might otherwise be devoted to resisting actively the restriction imposed by their society. This may well be the key to the reduced anxiety and hostility of the Zuni, which is less than would be expected from the high degree of control and inhibition which the social system exercises. Simple repression is also used as defense, but is greatly modified from what might be expected by the rich sublimation possibilities which the Zuni culture offers.

From these remarks it can be seen that while the Thematic Apperception test provides few surprises,because of what has already been learned from the other tests, it confirms and integrates the items found elsewhere.

Rorschach Test

The Rorschach tests were given and scored according to instructions in Klopfer and Kelley's The Rorschach Technique (1942). Since the figures derived from this method of scoring are highly technical and of interest only to Rorschach experts, they have not been included, and only interpretive remarks will be discussed here. The original protocols have been published on microcards (Leighton 1957: 2, 19).

As in most of the other tests, the Zuni children showed in the Rorschach test a marked tendency to conform to a tribal norm. This is not to say that there is no individual variation. Such variation is considerable, but it is less marked than in the other Indian tribes studied. The tendency toward conformity is more noticeable in the girls than in the boys, and the tribal pattern has already been established at the earliest age tested.

The Zuni children appear to be, on the whole, extremely well adjusted and self-sufficient. They have developed their inner resources and imaginations to a quite remarkable extent and seem to get great satisfaction from daydreaming and from the storymaking that this makes possible. They show evidence of being highly socialized and of having good control in relation to their personal interactions. They appear to have drawn a clear line between their own and white culture.

One of the most striking things about their records is the large amount of attention devoted to tiny details. Their absorption in these details is as marked as that found in obsessive-compulsive personalities in white culture. They show little interest in practical achievement as a main aim, but they attend to it to the extent of satisfying their own needs. However, there is no drive for achievement, practical or otherwise, as an end in itself.

They are strongly introverted and seem to spend all their intellectual energies on an elaborate in-group life. There is a rather marked conscious constraint. It appears that in most spheres of activity there are bounds over which they cannot step, but that within these bounds there is a reasonable amount of freedom. The Zuni appear in this test to be somewhat inflexible and resistant to change because of a sort of inner conviction and satisfaction with their own ways. One might expect, for example, that Zuni soldiers would absorb less from their experience in war than soldiers of some other tribes, and that they would return to their community comparatively little changed and able to settle back rather easily into the familiar ways.

While it is not possible to say what the changes in the Rorschach picture are for any given child at different age periods, there are certain contrasts between the four different age groups that may or may not hold for individuals. In the first place, there is an increasing concern with achievement and a decreasing proportion of attention paid to tiny details from the youngest group to the oldest. Secondly, there is a peak in the degree of spontaneity and the freedom from restraint at certain ages. For the girls, this is seen in the 11-13 year period and for the boys in the 8-10 year. Except for these peaks, reticence and passivity increase from the younger to the older groups. The one area in which control diminishes with age is that of the instinctual urges, which are doubtless sexual in nature. According to white Rorschach standards, this would mean that in respect to their inner urges, the Zuni children are less mature at 14-18 years than they are in the younger age groups. Obviously, this indicates that in this respect, the white measure of maturity and white sexual sanctions do not hold for the Zuni children. On the whole, there is a general trend from the youngest group to the oldest in the direction of what we have called the Zuni pattern, the youngest children being the farthest from it and the oldest group closest to it.

CHAPTER 12

"THE ZUNI CHILD" AND ZUNI CHILDREN

The preceding chapters have set forth the results of several tests applied to a sample group of Zuni children and have provided a number of com-
parisons between Zuni and white children or Zuni and other Indians. In order
to summarize these findings in an integrated way, an attempt will be made
here to describe the principal characteristics of "the Zuni child" as the tests
picture him. Such an attempt does violence, of course, to human individuality. However, it is common enough for a trader, anthropologist, or anyone
well acquainted with various Indians to be able to identify by tribe a strange
Indian, even without hearing him speak his native language or seeing distin-
guishing items of dress. Each tribe seems to develop in its members a sort of
gestalt of attitude and perhaps of behavior toward strangers which raises the
likelihood of recognition far above mere chance. From the test results reported in previous chapters, it seems probable that a Zuni would be easier to
recognize than certain other tribesmen because of the strong tendency toward
conformity.

Bearing in mind, then, that any given flesh-and-blood Zuni child may
present a number of exceptions to our description, let us see what can be said
about the composite "Zuni child."

By the time this child comes to school, he is already clearly marked
with the Zuni stamp. He will change a little as he grows older, and he will
vary in some attitudes and abilities according to whether he is a boy or a girl,
but there is no room for doubt that he is a Zuni.

He is in close touch with the real world, aware of its dangers and difficulties as well as its pleasures. Work is the main thing to do in the real world,
he thinks, especially work for the family. Work far outranks amusements,
school, religious observances, and everything else that was mentioned as a
good or bad thing to do. Closely related to work, though much lower in his
scale of values, come property and possessions, the receiving of which is the
best thing that could happen, and the loss of which is a cause of anger.

His social world is divided into two parts in the main: his family and outsiders. Outsiders are further divided into Zuni and others, with some gradations of various sorts among the others. The family and the Zuni (especially Zuni of the same age) fill most of the horizon for the school-age child. He is able to establish warm relations with some individuals. His family does three-quarters of the praising and blaming, with the parent of the same sex playing the largest part, since that parent is chiefly responsible for the child's training. Half of the people he associates with happiness and "best thing" are family members, while these members make up only one-quarter of the people associated with fear, anger, and shame. Agemates and "they" or "somebody" play the largest role in the "negative" emotions but rank far below the family for "positive" emotions. The child is especially sensitive to two aspects of interpersonal relations: first the sort of impression he makes on others (especially on nonfamily others), which easily arouses his embarrassment; and second his marked dislike for aggressiveness. The easy embarrassment leads him to pay considerable attention to what is expected of him and to follow the rules of his society. His antipathy to aggressiveness is probably in part a reflection of this conformity, but may also indicate that aggressive feelings against the various restraints upon him are rather strong.

Almost surely he is very much aware of the world of spirits, even though he does not talk much about it. The meeting ground between man and spirits, the tribal ceremonials, are a source of happiness for him. But for the most part he stands in fear of the supernatural beings and of the humans with supernatural power who might do him evil. He fears also the dark night and mysterious sounds and sights, because they remind him that dangerous spirits and people lurk everywhere.

What are the child's resources for dealing with his world? In the first place, he appears to be at least as intelligent as the average white child, even when this is measured by a test from white culture. In addition, he has a good imagination, which he uses quite freely. Somehow he has become convinced that to be a good Zuni is an aim worth striving for, and he has been willing to give up some of his autonomy in order to gain the approval of his family and society. He derives strong support from belonging to and participating in this best of all possible societies. He has found that life consists of a series of magic circles which set limits to what he can do in various lines of activity, but within which he is permitted some choice and freedom. These circles take care of all the big things in his life, leaving him only the arrangement and manipulation of details. By busying himself with what he is free to do, he uses up much of his energy and distracts his attention from his restrictions. One of these circles, which offers rich opportunities for sublimation, is that which encompasses the ceremonial life. Another is the practice of arts and crafts, and still another the area of making a living by farming and herding. The least restricting circle of all, perhaps, is the one defining sexual activities.

So much for "the Zuni child." The rest of the chapter attempts to show what some of the individual variations of this pattern are. The six children described were selected in conferences between Dr. Leighton and Mrs. Gonzales in an effort to represent as many as possible of the various Zuni cultural and economic factors. When the cases were discussed in Chicago, the complaint was made that they were too much alike. Accordingly, two or three of the most deviant children on the list were studied. But it was found that except in a few particulars, these children also largely conformed to the tribal pattern. The sketches will, therefore, be restricted to the six children originally chosen, because it seems that they display as well as any the range of differences. There is one boy and one girl to represent each of three age groups: the small children, the middle-sized children, and the oldest children. They are presented in order of age.

Amy

This little girl of seven was unique among the Zuni children in that she was the only one who took the trouble to learn Dr. Leighton's name and to greet her by name when they met around the school grounds. This made her appear more than usually friendly. Another outstanding feature about Amy was that she had mastered English better than most children of her age. She was said, moreover, to practice it outside of school and even at home, in which she was quite different from most of the other children. Her various teachers described her as a little busybody who would like to act constantly as a go-between for the teacher and the other pupils. She liked to manage both classroom and playground, and she was able to take charge of the classroom in the teacher's absence. On the playground, for example, she would decide the order in which children should use the slide, and she liked to be "it" when the game they were playing required such a character. She sometimes sulked if she could not be "it," and she sometimes pinched or slapped the other children to get her way. On the whole, however, her bossiness was intended to regulate the activity of others rather than to suppress it, and she seemed able to do this without angering the other children. Amy's older sister was also bossy, but was less successful in that other children were often irritated by her efforts to manage them. The position of these two girls in the school was reflected in the fact that when children in the group under study were told to draw a picture of someone, many of them drew either Amy or her sister.

With adults, Amy was quite amenable when compliance was insisted upon, but generally she seemed to disregard adult authority and to behave as seemed best to her rather than to accept authority willingly or reject it actively. About the only criticism of Amy was that she did not like to work at home and spent most of her time playing.

In appearance, Amy was an attractive, smiling, little girl, always very neat in her hair and dress and clean as to hands and face, although it was reported that her body cleanliness often left something to be desired. She started school as a visitor with her sister. She was currently in the first grade, and was said to be an excellent pupil. Her report showed that she had improved in every respect during her second year in school, and was rated "good" in all subjects.

Amy lived with her family and her maternal relatives in a three-room house which was rated in fair condition and moderately well kept up. This was the family's only residence, although Amy's father's family had a farm in one of the outlying villages, where the children sometimes went to visit and help with the harvest. The family income was low and was derived partly from the vegetable and livestock products which the father contributed, but mostly from the handwork done by the women. The household consisted of Amy and her parents, three sisters, of whom two were younger than Amy, a grandmother, four uncles, and two aunts. There was also a Navaho aunt-in-law, an uncle-in-law, and a baby cousin. All of the adults had had considerable schooling, and one of the aunts had been an extremely bright student. She was a very dominant personality and bossed the entire family. The household was described as being made up of dominant women and comparatively ineffectual men. Except for Amy's father, husbands in this family had been only transient members, and even Amy's father left home periodically, threatening never to return.

Amy acquired an IQ of 111 on the Arthur test and 93 on the Goodenough. This is the reverse of the expected relationship between these two tests among the Zuni. From the Thematic and the Rorschach tests, she appeared to have an intellectual ability that was "high average" or better. It is possible that her performance was not up to her capacity, since she was rather playful. She exercised considerable restraint over her spontaneity, and she was not very original or imaginative. She was rather careful and detailed in her observations and showed considerable organizing ability. She seemed to be slightly insecure about her interpersonal relations and wary of emotional situations. However, once she accepted such a situation, it stimulated her in a favorable way and she became very free and spontaneous in her emotions. There was no evidence of aggressiveness, but rather of a sensitiveness to the reactions of other people and a sort of executive drive. Her organizing ability, her sensitivity to other people, her easy emotionality, and her lack of aggressiveness ought to make her something of a leader among her agemates. She was greatly dominated by adults, particularly the females of her family group. There was evidence of some hidden difficulty and apprehension about this, for she apparently reacted to their attitude by rather timid obedience. Their forcefulness seems to have frightened Amy somewhat. Perhaps it was in reaction to this that she refused to work at home and ran outside to play, as the family complained.

Charles

Charles, at eight and a half, was an up-and-coming little chap, responsive and likeable, but with a quick temper and a little smart-alecky at times. However, he was not hard to control if he understood that he had to behave. Like Amy, he also wanted to be the leader of his group. For example, when he and other little boys came to school early and sat in the back of the room reading together, Charles always wanted to play teacher. He got along well with the others and was quite popular, though he tended to lose his temper if his leadership was questioned. At home, quarrels among the brothers and sisters usually began with Charles.

He had reached the third grade in school and was accounted an excellent pupil. He seemed to like school, always came on time, and looked as though someone had helped him get ready each morning. He was responsive and interested in his work. His English was good, he liked to read, and he took active part in games. He was not as good with his hands as with his head.

Charles lived with his parents, two brothers, and two sisters, in a nice three-room house on the outskirts of the village. Three older male cousins and a grandfather also shared these quarters. The house was well kept and contained a number of modern conveniences. Running water was soon to be added at the time of interviewing. The father went away from Zuni for his schooling, and the mother finished sixth grade on the reservation. As is characteristic of the younger educated parents, this pair was interested in their children's school progress.

The father worked industriously on his fifteen irrigated acres and superintended his flock of sheep. He spent less time idling about the village than many of the men. His interest and participation in the Zuni religious life was probably about average, and he did not hold any special position. The mother not only had time to take excellent care of her house and family but also did a good deal of silver work, which helped to pay the store bills. Together, the parents made a good living for the family, probably about average for Zuni. In addition to a fair amount of furniture and farm tools, they owned a reasonably good collection of Zuni jewelry.

Charles was second in the family. His older brother had nearly all the good qualities that Charles had, but was quieter, did not get into as much mischief, and was easier to handle. Since he skipped a grade in school, he had not done quite as good school work as before, probably because of missing a year's instruction. Next younger than Charles was a girl who seemed quite backward during her first two years of school, but later improved a good deal.

At the time of the study the two older boys helped their mother quite a bit with the housework, as there was no sister old enough to do this.

All the children in the family were nursed until the birth of the next child, when they were weaned. All were said to have cried a good deal as infants. All were kept on a cradleboard and slept with their parents until the next baby came, when they were moved to another bed. When visited, Charles and the other boy had one bed, the parents had another, the sister had a third, and the baby slept in a crib. The family emotional atmosphere appeared to be harmonious, but a little on the impersonal side. This was the only marriage for each parent, and gave promise of being a permanent one.

In spite of the good impression that Charles made in school, he attained only an average IQ on both the intelligence tests--99 on the Arthur and 105 on the Goodenough. Both the Rorschach and the Thematic Apperception tests indicated that his intellectual capacity was somewhat higher than his achievement on the intelligence tests, but that he used this ability in a way which was not very productive. He confined himself to analysis and observation, and did little in the way of putting things together. At the same time, in his studies these various qualities might well work together to create a good impression. He carried to an extreme the general Zuni tendency to pay attention to tiny details. Imagination and originality were not given much scope. He avoided to some extent coming to grips with practical reality or with emotional relationships by a sort of impersonal intellectualizing. It was apparent that he was quite vigorous and managerial and that he probably got along well with people in a superficial way. He showed no tendency to avoid people, but only to avoid emotional relationships with them. It appeared that this uneasiness about emotional relationships might stem from some lack of warmth in his early experience with his parents. At the current stage he was a remarkably introspective little boy and betrayed by this and by other means a feeling of insecurity and uneasiness which did not, however, amount to a marked anxiety. It seemed likely that as he grew older he would find a more satisfactory mode of adjustment than he had so far achieved.

Clara

This ten-year-old girl was able to produce the following autobiography, which gives some of her views on her past experiences.

Story of Myself

I was born in September. I was born in Zuni, McKinley County, New Mexico.

My mother and father are living. My grandmother died.

When I was little I play with dolls. My dolls were not American dolls, they were some kind of dance doll.

I play tag and the cat and the mice. Sometimes I play duck the ball and I like to run rabbit run the best.

I like to play jacks at school. I don't run fast when I get tired. Last Thursday I run with Lucy and Katie, I didn't run fast and I got tired.

We have chief dance and rain dances and many other dances. That is all I will tell about the dances.

Now I am big to learn about everything in school. Soon the school will be out and we are practicing to high jump.

Now I will tell you about my friends and their names are Susie, Louisa, Ella, and Olive. My best friends are Agnes and Connie. Agnes is a fast runner and she can jump as high.

I have many brothers and sisters. There are six of us and one sister make two sisters. Now they are going to sheep camp soon as school is out. My mother is planting vegetables in her garden. Many Zuni women are planting to eat in the winter.

We have a Shlake [Shalako] house and had five rooms in it. We got lots of food and had a feast. At Shlake we have many friends and they give us some that they can make us happy. When Shlake is over we plant feathers and pray.

The Zuni girls dance doll dance and also the boys dance too. When the doll dance is over there is much crowded that when you go home you will be lost.

The Zuni Indians bake bread in the ovens. Sometimes we bake paper bread in the hot stone. And we cooked chili bread and corn bread.

My little brother is a funny baby and can make other people make them happy. He can play in the sunshine. We study about healthy and geography too.

We will have a track meet soon and I am happy because school is soon be out. And everybody is glad too. Ella, Edna, Lucy, and Mina are fast runners. Last week Ella's mother was a fast runner and they put Ella in. I am not a fast runner last week. Now I am not good runner now. Soon we are going to sheep camp and plant and watch the sheep. When I was a little girl I watch sheep too. But now I am old to help cook the food. Soon we are going to cam

Clara was an attractive little girl, though rather thin and a bit on the shy side. She tended to be quiet and got along well with the girls in her room, but was not especially popular. She was very much interested in reading and writing, even to the extent of taking books home to read. She was in the fourth grade during the year of the study. In a grade which contained a number of bright children, Clara was still outstanding intellectually, although she was not as good at hand work of various kinds as were some of the others. There had been a steady improvement in her school record from the time she started as a beginner: her first year was rated as "average," the next two years "good," and the past two years "excellent."

When Clara first came to school she was extremely shy, rather babyish, and seemed to have been spoiled. However, by the time she reached the fourth grade she had outgrown this, was respectful and responsive, easy to handle in school, and obedient and willing to shoulder her responsibilities at home. Clara lived with her large family in a very good five-room house, which had been built recently to entertain the Shalako, as she said. The house was comfortably furnished, had running water, and was very well kept. Their forty-acre farm, flock of sheep, and the silverwork and beadwork of the women provided a comfortable living. Clara's family included her parents and five brothers. She was the fourth child. In the house also lived a half-sister and her husband and child, two cousins and their husbands, and three second cousins. These cousins were all related through the mother. The parents had not gone to school, but all other members of the household who were old enough had done so. Some had even been away to boarding school.

This whole group was said to be somewhat like Clara, quiet and well-behaved. They were considered a good, stable family and held a fairly important place in the Zuni cultural community. Since the parents spoke no English, they were represented to the whites by the oldest educated daughter, but were probably the real powers in the household. Although the family might have been considered conservative in that they played an important part in Zuni religious life and formed a large matrilocal group, which was no longer the universal pattern at Zuni, they had always been very cooperative with white people.

Clara and her brothers were all nursed until the next baby came, when they had to learn to do without this. They all walked before they talked and were rather slow in learning to talk. They were still somewhat reticent when it came to speaking. Each shared his parents' bed until he was displaced by the next child. Toilet training was accomplished by the usual Zuni method of taking the child outdoors and helping him until he learned to do it for himself, and was completed without any particular trouble. The children did not present any disciplinary problem. The boys in the family had been less outstanding scholastically than Clara, but still they did good work. They kept busy on the farm and at the sheep camp. In school they were good athletes. By contrast, as Clara herself says, she was not a very good athlete. It seemed that good interpersonal relations in this family were rather taken for granted and lacked the warmth that one might have expected in such a close unit. However, it may be merely that they were less demonstrative than some other families.

On the tests, Clara earned an IQ of 104 on the Arthur and 134 on the Goodenough. The higher score tallies better with her teachers' opinions and with her performance on the Thematic Apperception and Rorschach tests than does the lower one. While there was nothing adverse noted on her health record, teachers said that she frequently complained of feeling tired, or of her stomach hurting, and that she acted nervous at times. She showed the expected Zuni interest in details and in analytical thinking and the lack of interest in synthesis and achievement. She used her imagination and originality to a considerable extent, and a good deal of fantasy was evident. Basically, she was rather self-assertive, but she exercised a conscious control over this as well as over most of her other impulses. She seemed to be much more restrained in her reaction to the world about her than in the use of her imagination and of fantasy, which again is what one expects to find in a Zuni. She showed more sophistication and maturity for a child of her age than many of the Indian children. The influence of white culture was quite evident in her choice of concepts. Her spontaneity and freedom of action were considerably limited by the type of conscious control which she exercised. However, she appeared to be a vigorous and active girl who should get along satisfactorily with her agemates. She had the kind of sense of humor that should make her a delightful person socially, but lacked the empathic quality that makes for closeness of emotional ties. Probably when she grows older and more sure of herself she will be able to relax her control a little and make the most of her excellent endowments.

Peter

Peter, at twelve, was a lively, talkative boy who was well liked by everyone. He was the first to arrive at school in the morning, and spent his noon hour at school also, never going home for lunch. He took part in a great deal of friendly scuffling with the other boys, even in the classroom after classes. He was something of a leader among the smart group in his class, who were prone to laugh readily at the mistakes of others. Peter himself was somewhat sensitive to criticism and tended to sulk when rebuked. On the playground, however, he was a good sport.

He started school in the kindergarten and was retained there for one-and-a-half years. There was such a steady improvement in his school work that later he was skipped from the third to the fifth grade. He was said to be particularly good with his hands, excelling in shopwork and art work. He was always eager to tackle new things, but was also willing to repeat what he had already done. His latest teacher considered him above average in mentality.

Peter was the third of three children. He lived with his parents, his older brother and sister, and two male cousins in a three-room house in Zuni or a two-room house in one of the farming villages. Their better-than-average income was derived chiefly from farming and livestock. The mother and sister did a little beadwork. Both Peter and his sister had been outstanding students in school, although the sister was extremely shy and quiet. The older brother, on the other hand, was not thought to be very bright, perhaps because he had a hearing defect. Neither of the parents had gone to school and they spoke no English. They were not outstanding in the community in any way, but took a conservative part in the religious life. They did not make any show of their prosperity, wearing clothes appropriate to a lower income group.

The family atmosphere seemed to be congenial and close. The parents were interested in the children and were aware of their individual problems. They apparently talked over family affairs with the children and would send word by Peter to the school principal or the teacher about when they planned to go to their farm and such matters.

Although the two older children were nursed as infants, Peter was raised on goat's milk, because his mother had trouble with her breasts. Like his sister, he talked before he walked, but instead of becoming quiet and reserved as she has, Peter never stopped talking. Toilet training took place at about three years and was guided by the mother. All the children slept with their parents as infants. Later the two boys were put in one bed and the girl in another. They all dreamed and talked in their sleep a good deal, but since they all talked English, the mother did not know what they said. They had always been obedient and industrious, with no disciplinary problems. They quarreled occasionally, but never fought. They never really played, preferring to sit and look at magazines when not working. Peter had never been off the reservation.

Although his teachers always thought of Peter as "delicate," or not very strong, health examination failed to reveal anything except some undernourishment. He earned an IQ of 107 on the Arthur test and 108 on the Goodenough. This was not quite as high as the teacher's estimate nor quite what the Rorschach test and the Thematic Apperception would indicate as to his capacity. His ability was less one-sided than that of many of the children described. From all the tests, Peter appeared to be one of the best rounded and least inhibited children studied. He showed more interest in practical matters than is characteristic of Zuni children, and a good balance between the use of his imagination, creativity, and inner resources and his approach to the outer world. He was both sensitive to and responsive to other people, although he was not unduly dependent on them. There was no evidence of anxiety or inhibition, and, in general, he seemed to be a relaxed type of child. This was reflected also in the judgment of the teachers, who described him as a "natural" child. About the only difficulty that one might forecast for Peter would be that the strict control exercised by Zuni society might hamper him when he grew older.

Angela

Angela was a sixteen-year-old high school senior. She was an attractive young woman who seemed to be always working. After school she frequently did odd jobs for the teachers or other white people in the village. Angela had such a good reputation for dependability and accuracy that she was selected from the other school girls to fill a government position at Zuni. Although she was considered a little "standoffish" in her personal relationships, she had a name for politeness with both whites and Zuni adults, and she got along quite well with the other girls, in spite of having only one intimate friend.

In school she had made a good impression also, although she was by no means the best student in school. She had been universally marked "very good" as a general evaluation. Her school performance became more consistent as she grew older, and she would generally stick with an assignment until she got it right.

The family's only residence was a good five-room house, very neatly kept, in Zuni village. Recently it had been partly rebuilt to entertain the Shalako. This house was shared by sixteen persons, of whom six were Angela's immediate family and the rest maternal relatives and their husbands and children. Family ties were said to be very close, and matrilocal residence was observed; thus the grandparents were always a part of the household, and the grandmother particularly had a hand in Angela's early training. The family was quite important in Zuni religious life and also had a reputation for being friendly and cooperative with white people. As a group, they seemed to be above average intellectually and economically. They were more up-and-coming than most Zunis and showed a greater tendency than the average to seek jobs working for white people. Although the grandparents and parents had had no schooling, the younger members of the mother's generation and all of Angela's generation have had considerable education.

The mother was a pleasant woman, who was quite willing to be interviewed about the children. An educated sister acted as interpreter and the grandmother assisted in recalling details of Angela's childhood. Care was taken to exclude the children who were being discussed from the room, and the interviewers were requested not to repeat what was said to either of the girls. The father was a man of some importance in his own right, who contributed to the family income by farming and sheep raising. He had been married previously, and his first family had been raised by his first wife's relatives.

The mother and the grandmother recalled that Angela, the fourth of five children, was nursed for about a year and a half and objected a good deal to the weaning process. She did not walk until she was about two, and by that time was already talking. She was rather slow in learning to keep herself clean. She was eager to go to school and had always been interested in it. She had started dancing in the religious ceremonials some time ago, participating quite frequently. When she was little, her grandmother took most of the care of her and spoiled her, just as she did all the other children. Her mother is proud of this girl's ability to take charge of the household when necessary. Angela's own recollection of her childhood can be found in her autobiography:

Story of My Life

The people that were in my family at the time of my birth were: my grandmother, grandfather, father, two sisters, one brother, aunts, and two uncles. I was born in the Zuni pueblo. During my early life I first remember that my grandfather and grandmother took me to the Peach Orchard to look after the peaches. This is the time when I was about two years of age, I enjoyed staying up there. After I came down to Zuni the children that I played with then were my neighborhood children and some of them were my nieces and cousins. The things that we play were hide and seek, play dolls and we went swimming in the river and for time being we played different kinds of games.

When I was five years of age I played most of the time, but when I was old enough to do some little things around the house my mother taught me how to take care of my sister, and my aunt used to teach me how to wash dishes carefully and not drop them and broke them. At the time when I was seven years old my folks use to take me to the sheep camp at lambing time. This is the place where I use to like best in my early days of my life. The reason I like this place best because I use to play with the little orphan lambs and goats, and at shearing time I use to go around the corrals and pick up some bits of wool that have

been left on the ground while shearing the sheep.
When I pick them up I put them in a sugar sack and
when I come home from camp I use to sell the wool.
I bought me some candy.

The good times I have had was when going on a
trip with the school children, and the bad things that
had happened that I still remember now is when they
had a deep snow. It sure did make me worried because lots of the Zuni women and men were out in the
forest picking piñons and also my folks were out in the
forest, too. There was lots of sheep damaged and one
man died coming home. This is the bad thing that has
happened that I still can remember.

And then the first dance that I had took part in it
was the Doll Dance. This dance usually comes in the
fall.

The school I'm now going is the Zuni Day School
which I like best, because I think I can get everything
out of it than the two schools we have round here in
Zuni. The best friend I have in school is Viola. We
treat each other as sisters. We have been friends ever
since we were kids.

The sickness that I have had was measles. I have
this sickness when I was three years old and I don't
know how it was cure.

I don't go to church on Sundays, but during every
Wednesday afternoons one of the Preachers from Mission school comes over and teach us about the real living God. This is the Protestant Preacher. I never did
go to any other churches. This summer I will have to
work in the office. I will work in this office when I
finished school and this is the only thing I can do.

The average family I have now is about fifteen.
The people in it are my three sisters, two brother-in-
law, aunt, grandmother, mother, father, uncle, three
nephews, one cousin, and one niece. The family is
large but most of the time we get along just fine and
once in a great while we get after the little ones if
they don't behave theirselves.

One that scolds me when I do wrong things is my
mother. She scolds me when I do wrong things because she don't want me to be naughty as a little child.

She got the right to get after me because it's good to
be straighten out. The person that gives me presents
and treats me nicely is my grandmother. She is the
one that took care of me when I was young. The only
thing I can do to earn my living when I get old enough
is to find a permanent job and earn money instead of
being a lazy person. I think this is the only way I can
earn my living. It's hard to tell whether I'm going to
do it or not.

Based on the foregoing, it is no surprise to learn that Angela achieved
an IQ of 128 on the Arthur test. She was too old for the Goodenough. Estimates of her intelligence from the Thematic Apperception and the Rorschach
were not quite so high, but were superior. She seemed to have more drive
for achievement than is expected with the Zuni children, and, as is the case
when the children grow older, she paid more attention to practical matters.
There was also evidence in her record of the somewhat compulsive attention
to small details that is so common in Zuni children. She seemed to exercise
a very strict conscious control over both her inner life and her outer reactions.
Spontaneity and freedom of action were thus low. She appeared to take very
seriously the Zuni values of hard work and restraint. She was rather highly
conventional, with relatively little imagination and originality. The one
sphere in which she seemed to be comparatively unrestrained was the sexual,
but even here she appeared not to have made up her mind whether to give in
to her impulses wholeheartedly or to reject them.

Frank

Frank, at seventeen years of age, was an attractive, well-dressed
tenth grader. He did not push himself forward, but was very willing to do
anything he was asked. He was a good athlete, good at his studies, and very
good at art work. He took responsibility well and was popular with both
teachers and students. His mates found him a good fellow, loyal and depend-
able. The girls liked him also, but he did not pay very much attention to
them. When occasionally he got into mischief, he was very shamefaced
afterward and surprised that he should have done such a thing. Following his
father's death, when Frank was sixteen, he took on a good deal of the family
responsibility and his mother came to depend on him.

He had been rated an "excellent" or outstanding pupil ever since he
had been coming to school, and at the time of the study he was considered
one of the best students in the entire enrollment.

The family had a very neatly-kept home in Zuni and an outlying ranch where they did their farming and sheep raising. Their exact financial status was not known, but all the children in the family dressed rather better than the average. Both parents had been married before, and each had children who currently felt almost as close to each other as if they had been full brothers and sisters. This is quite unusual in Zuni. They were a very affectionate group. The home was shared by Frank and his mother, two brothers and two sisters, a half-brother, a half-sister and her husband, and a great uncle.

Neither parent was educated, but the children had all had considerable schooling. The mother seemed to be a pleasant woman, very fond of all her children. She let the last child nurse until he went to school. She did most of the training of her children, with a little help from her mother and a good deal from Frank and his next younger brother. She said that all the children crawled about on the floor before they walked. This is unusual for Zuni babies, who usually pass directly from the lap to walking. Each was weaned when the next child arrived. All the children made a good impression in school, but Frank was definitely the most outstanding of the group. The elder of his two sisters had always been the most difficult of the children to handle, but still had not presented much of a problem. She had nightmares and talked in her sleep almost every night. Frank and his brother had traveled more widely than was common with the school children because of their activity with the basketball team. They had been to Albuquerque, Crownpoint, Fort Apache, Fort Wingate, and Gallup.

Frank's own account of his life gives a good idea of the things that had impressed him most:

> In the first place I really don't know everything from my cradle and up to now but I will try my best to write every bit of it. Most all of my folks are with me except my father leave me last year, which I didn't think it was going to happen.
>
> I was born right here in pueblo of Zuni. Of course my folks moved out of the old house where I was borned.
>
> The first thing I could remember was the water in the reservoir at the hill ranch. I used to see the ducks swim around the lake. Of course I didn't even know they were ducks then. After I had got up on my feet, I had lot of friends to play with. We used to go hunting birds with slingshots or go swimming which was my favorite sports.
>
> When I was old enough my father took me out to the field where he used to let me ride on plow as he move along. As he took me every day out to the field he might have thought that I knew well enough to put some

seeds in the row. He let me do it. He told me to put
so many seeds in as he went along. I start counting
seeds and drop them in and go slowly along until he
catch up with me again that the horses almost step on
my heels. He has to stop and wait on me until I got
used to it.

I usually live at the ranch during summer and in
winter time I live in Zuni. At the ranch I take care of
the farm and herd sheep and help round up the cattle.
I like the hill ranch better because there where I live
most of the time and there lots of things which would
make you feel happy and lot of things to do.

Surely I had lot of good times and bad times during
my born days. One time I almost did drown when I
went swimming in the river. I didn't know it was so
deep. I went in there and the next thing I knew I was
slowly going in then I call for help. All the children
I was with them run away then I finally got to side of
the river I grab the brush that was near by I got out.

I didn't think of dances were important then because I knew nothing about, but after I had been initiated and danced for myself. The first dance I danced
in was Comanche. It was during the winter night dance,
but the time I got to the last house I was sure tired.
After that I never had dance very often just once in
while to know that I'm initiated.

I have been learning every bit of my education in
Zuni Day School. I haven't be roaming around every
school to see what they look like and what work they
do. I think in one school you attend you should stay
then that way anyone could learn more. I think Zuni
Day School is the best place where there's lot of new
things to learn for my future life.

My friends now are pretty nice to me, they have
been treating me fine.

I don't know what I like to be best now best thing
for me to do now is to plow all my fields.

I don't know what kind of sickness I had when I was
little and how they were cured. After all I haven't been
having trouble with sickness.

Of course I don't go to church any place.

This summer I would like to do some plowing and
help roundup the cattle.

Best thing for me to do when I finish school or before
I finish school is to go serve for my country if the war
isn't over.

We have quite a large family, my mother, three
sister, three brothers, and four nephews. We get along
fine all the times that is the big folks but the kids fight
and scold each others. I think nobody scold me when I
do wrongs things which I have never done in my boyhood,
but when I was little my father used to spank me and I
knew it was for my own goods, so I won't do it again.
I think I will earn my living by farming or by some
government jobs.

Frank achieved an IQ of 137 in the Arthur Point Performance scale. Although at his age this score does not give an adequate evaluation of his ability,
it is ample justification of his standing in the school. The Rorschach and
Thematic Apperception tests rated him "unquestionably superior." Frank used
his intellectual ability chiefly for brilliant observation and imaginative elaboration. He seemed to have little interest in organization, in fantasy, or in
intellectual achievement for its own sake. He had made a very smooth emotional adjustment, but he was more reactive to outside stimulation than he was
spontaneous. He exerted a rather high degree of conscious and intellectual control over all his reactions, but this was modified both by sensitivity to his social
environment and by introspection. Like Angela, he seemed to be greatly impressed with the Zuni values of restraint and obedience, and he carried out these
values conscientiously. There was some evidence that Frank was a little uneasy
lest he be unable to keep up to the ideals held up to him by his mother. No
doubt his father's death and his own assumption of responsibility had contributed
to this feeling of unease. As was seen for the oldest group of Zuni children as
a whole, Frank showed the somewhat exaggerated development of instinctual
drives which probably represents unrepressed sexuality.

It is easy to see in these six children how many personality traits are
shared, how many of the cultural traits described in Part I are common to all
the families. Yet each is unique in his particular constellation and patterning
of these traits. Factors tending to produce such uniformity include the isolation
of the Zuni group, with consequent in-breeding and the homogeneity of the
culture. Thus, children with extensively shared heredity are reared by generally accepted techniques to take their places in a well-established and
clearly defined culture, where a rather strict conformity is expected of all.
The wonder and the consolation is that human individuality persists, even if
in a limited way, in the face of such heavy pressures against it.

CHAPTER 13

THE CHANGING PUEBLO—CONCLUSIONS AND EXPECTATIONS

The testing program has given a picture of Zuni personality which can
be viewed against the backdrop of the cultural environment described in Part I.
The anthropologist has drawn his picture of life at Zuni from firsthand observation and from reports in the literature. In Part II, another dimension has been
added to our understanding of the Zuni people by means of the psychological
conceptions of Zuni personality derived from the interpretation of more or less
standardized tests.

Both the anthropologists' and the psychologists' findings point up the
fact that the Zuni individual learns his code of behavior as a result of strong
social pressures. These are mediated chiefly by his family until he is old
enough to go about alone in the pueblo, when the full force of the attitude of
other Zuni toward him begins to drive home the lessons taught by the family.
The extended family on both sides plays an important part, as well as the
parents themselves.

The most positive value is placed on work and industry. That this is
so can be learned both from the psychological battery of tests and from the
anthropological literature. The value of work in cooperation with others is
constantly drummed into the children. It runs through the folklore, is evi-
denced in the archaeology, and is constantly demonstrated in field and ceremony. Of the six children described, Amy avoids work still, Charles is beginning to do his part, Peter and Clara seem to have regular responsibilities,
while Angela and Frank evidently regard work as the natural way for a person
to spend his time. Except for Amy, there is no sign of dislike for work, and
in her case her attitude may be a mixture of her youth and a certain resistance
by an "executive type" to being bossed.

The basic value of hard work has been all-important in the survival
of the Zuni in a harsh agricultural environment. Or, stated the other way
around, survival has been possible only through cooperative effort, and that

has come to be valued above all else. The Zuni believes that crops are grown by ritual as well as by hoe. Cooperation and hard work is therefore demanded not only in the field but also in the kiva and on the dance plaza. In a certain respect the Zuni is perfectly right, for it has been primarily through the compulsive attention to ritual that he has related himself to his brother Zuni in cooperative endeavor, which has preserved the social whole and perpetuated man as well as his crops. From the Zuni point of view, the reliving of the myths of the people in mass ritual carried on year after year, generation after generation, has had the desired effect: the Katchina ancestors and the gods have blessed them with rain and food.

Of course the white man, with different religious values, does not believe that Zuni ritual directly affects the natural elements. His science argues against such belief. But when he attempts to analyze man's relation to man, either by tests or by deduction from observed behavior, he notes that Zuni behavior, enforced by religious belief, has brought about a set of coordinated actions that have tended to tie man to man and to the rest of the social whole. He notes, furthermore, that these relationships have functioned to perpetuate the society and culture. This explanation of pueblo continuity, which, to be sure, has depended on crop production, does not subscribe to the Zuni's own simple causal and mechanistic explanation, that if the ritual is correctly performed, the rain will come and corn will grow. But it does take account of the fact that group rituals have had a direct function in perpetuating the social whole. The white scientist concludes that it has been the high degree of cooperation of the Zuni in their social and ritual groupings that has perpetuated Zuni culture in the face of great odds. The Zuni, imbued with their religious explanations, believe that it is these ritual acts themselves, performed by men of good heart, that have given them food and life throughout the years.

Part II emphasizes in particular two aspects of interpersonal relations: shame as a technique of social control and an abhorrence of aggression. Zuni more than any other of the Indian groups studied (Navaho, Sioux, Papago, Zia, and Hopi) were easily embarrassed before others. The Zuni children were greatly concerned with the sort of appearance they made and with maintaining smooth relationships with other people. All the children testified that aggression by others, more than any other human cause, made them angry, while the boys stated that the worst thing that could happen to them was to display their own aggression. It is made clear in the cultural analysis that these attitudes carry over into adulthood.

Zuni, then, is an outstanding example of a "shame" culture. It is this psychological trait that accounts for the "social timidities" mentioned so often by Elsie Clews Parsons, and this trait, plus the feeling about aggression, that gives rise to the "Apollonian" behavior described by Ruth Benedict. Sensitivity to the actions and opinions of others makes each Zuni highly vulnerable to ridicule and gossip. His own anger and aggression is not allowed to find a direct outlet, but is sublimated in the form of counter-gossip, witchery, and the group ritual that affords a safety valve to the individual and the community.

Administrators of pueblo affairs and teachers in the Zuni schools, as well as some social scientists, have been puzzled by Benedict's picture of pueblo personality and culture. Their experience with the Zuni does not conform to her Apollonian ideal. They see the ceremonial whippings of the children, the threatenings and constant fear of witches, the gossip, and the ostracism of certain individuals as being contrary to the picture she has painted of the Zuni life-way. Certain of the ceremonies of the curing societies might qualify better as "Dionysian" behavior. Certainly it was true that in 1946 and 1947, when some two hundred veterans returned to the pueblo, behavior was anything but Apollonian. Witchcraft was rampant. Whites were asked to leave the pueblo, and suspicion ran high. Anyone who observed Zuni at this particular time would certainly side with the "Dionysian" school of thought, and feel that Benedict was completely wrong in her interpretation. One social scientist has gone so far as to say that these two schools of thought cannot be reconciled. Both sides can quote evidence for their interpretations. However, if one examines pueblo cultural continuity with the picture of Zuni personality as presented in Part II in mind, he will find that this apparent contradiction can be explained.

On the one hand, the Zuni does seek the middle way--he does avoid aggression in others and sublimate it in himself; on the other, he does threaten and punish and repress, he is a vicious gossip, and on occasion there are epidemics of witchcraft. The missing ingredient in the either/or argument is time perspective. This may be pointed up by quoting a Zuni informant who said, in speaking of the 1920s and early '30s (in which period Benedict made her study): "Zuni wasn't as troubled then as it is now [1947]. The people didn't go into town with autos. The priests didn't quarrel with each other."

Benedict described a well-functioning culture before it had been brought into close contact with the "outside." The prolonged contacts with the teachers (who now are educating a third and in some cases a fourth generation of school children in the American way), the missionaries, the traders, and the government workers, and, most of all, the contacts of the Indians with Gallup and other Southwestern towns, have all tended to modify the picture of Zuni as it existed thirty years ago. Or, to put it in social science language, the acculturating process has accelerated during these years. This process, it should be pointed out, has left its mark both on the individual (personality) and on the group (culture). The trouble with Benedict's picture of Zuni is not so much her facts as the limitations of her theory, which is one of flat configuration, one that did not allow sufficiently for culture change.

These contacts with the outside, the veteran's experience in World War II, the pre-War stock reduction program, and the technological advances which have been introduced to the pueblo have all tended to upset the Apollonian balance, allowing the other aspect of Zuni personality to become more prominent. It is almost like a coin with contrasting pictures on opposite sides. But the important thing to remember is that they are both designs on a single coin, which cannot be properly described without taking account of both. In times of crisis the aggressive behavior that is usually sublimated breaks out into the open and is manifested in drunkenness, witchery, and political feuding. Those who have been in the pueblo during such a period of tension have marveled that the town did not blow up. Other pueblos, the Hopi villages for example, during periods of great stress have broken up into smaller groups. Thus, Hotevilla budded off from Oraibi. That Zuni has never split up into smaller groups is probably due in part to the intersecting lines of social relations that each individual has. Kiva group, own clan, father's clan, and membership in a curing society all have different planes of cleavage, binding each person to many others.

There are also safety valves which help the Zuni "let off steam." The most evident of these are: the group rituals, which tend to restore balance for the community; the curing ceremonies, which tend to restore the equilibrium of the individual; and the annual migration of many families out of the pueblo to their farms. By means of these various valves, much of the tension is dissipated. A case of social adjustment that laid bare some of these Zuni techniques occurred in 1946-47, when the veterans of World War II returned to the pueblo. They brought back with them a way of life that was quite foreign to Zuni: They spoke English in public places, wore clothes that identified them as American soldiers rather than as Zuni, and in some instances openly scoffed at the religion of the elders. The reaction of the older residents was just what one would expect: there was a good deal of gossip about the deviant behavior of these men. The old sensitivity to ridicule had not been dulled by brief residence away from home. Within a few years these soldiers either were brought back into line or left the pueblo to live elsewhere. During this time the level of anxiety in the village was high; many of the elders thought that these men, who were no longer "pure in heart," would cause drought. But as such gossip mounted, more veterans took part each year in the dances, "just to keep gossip down," as some said, or so that their parents "would not be ashamed" of them. Thus, the group anxiety was largely assuaged and by 1948 the pueblo was running smoothly again.

Similarly, the anxiety of the individual during this period of readjustment was effectively treated by the shamans. Some of the elders thought that the unsettled behavior of their sons was caused by witches and insisted that curers be called in to suck out the illness. Many veterans went through such ceremonies, and many were prepared for initiation into the Cult of the Beast Gods.

The farming villages also promote stability. Each spring, a good portion of the winter population breaks up into smaller groups, and tensions are relaxed in the larger community. The autobiographies of Clara, Angela, and Frank express real enjoyment of the time spent out of Zuni village. An experienced government worker is convinced that new programs are likely to be better accepted if introduced in the summer rather than in the late winter, when the pueblo is usually more tense.

This building up of tension during the winter and spring and its subsequent release in the summer months is a pueblo phenomenon especially worthy of note at Zuni. During the late spring, the winds blow. In Zuni rationale this is caused by witches. At this time of year there is also mounting concern over the crops: Will there be enough moisture in the soil? Will the rains come? Once the farmers disperse to the fields and busy themselves with planting their crops, and the Uwanami go into retreat prior to starting the summer dances, the anxiety subsides.

If an individual does not wish to conform to the group but aspires to live "like a white man," he may do so, providing he leaves the reservation. The Zuni individualist finds it more pleasant, if he wants to vary from the norm, to be away from the pueblo, free from gossip and social pressure. He goes to Gallup or elsewhere to live as he wants. Zuni history is full of instances of such self-imposed exile. As a result, acculturation of the pueblo is slower than it would be if the most "progressive" individuals chose to face up to criticism of their conduct and continue to live in the village. But pueblo history is also a testament to the failure of the Zuni individual to compete economically on the outside. Many of the exiles return, embittered, chastened, and reactionary to white ways. The ultraconservative Zuni leader often has had such a period of unsuccessful struggle with life away from the village.

Let us now speculate about the future. Today, strange to say, the Sun Priest, one of the most sacred and important of the priests, has moved to Gallup. Many of his duties have lapsed, and it will be difficult if not impossible to get another incumbent for the office. To be a faithful and attentive Pekwin is a full-time job, whose principal reward is virtue and prestige. This situation clashes with the interests of the young men, who in an earlier day in pueblo history would have been candidates for this priesthood, but who are now oriented toward a wage economy. So too for the Bow Priests. This priesthood will probably have no incumbents after the death of the present Bow Priest. Much of the Zuni ceremony will lapse if these two offices become extinct.

Work for wages, whether it be for the trader as a silversmith or in town as a common laborer or skilled mechanic, runs counter to Zuni life-ways but still becomes more and more general. The old power structure that was present when Zuni was a true theocracy is bound to change. Social relations and social control will also change, and a new power structure will emerge, based probably more on economic and social relations than on ritual ones.

Ceremonies will be carried on, possibly for generations. Certainly the whole religious system will not tumble overnight. But when there is no longer anxiety over the amount of rainfall as the key to survival, the dances will be performed without the "religious thrill" that was once there. As one informant put it, "Shalako will become just like your Christmas." Nor will there be the incentive to bring rain for the crops. Why grow crops at all if you can earn money to buy food in the store?

In all probability, the strong Zuni shame psychology will alter as the social pressures change and as American individualism takes hold. The religion of the people, which was once so functional in a closely-knit agricultural community, will not be functional in an ethnic group which finds itself more and more in contact with the greater society. As individualism grows, so too will the prestige of the curers, whose therapy will be supportive for the Zuni individual in a rapidly changing world beset with conflicts. Furthermore, the Zuni who loses his shame sanctions as the closely-knit social structure loosens up may develop the conscience and sense of guilt that is the technique of control of the larger society. Then he will be more susceptible to the advances of the missionaries.

This is not just loose speculation. "Primitive" communities in Africa and in the South Seas, and various "primitive" peoples in Asia and South America have gone through similar transformations of personality and culture. We have this comparative data to guide us in our understanding of future change at Zuni. But who will be so brave as to say when the Zuni will, as a group, be thrown completely out of their orbit by the outward force? Who would be so rash as to pinpoint even the half century when there will no longer be the counteracting centripetal force of the Middle Place?

FOOTNOTES

1. For a detailed breakdown of this acreage as to land status, date of acquisition, and authority for acquisition, see Aberle 1948: 83, Table I (S).

2. For an excellent description of the Zuni topography upon which this description is based, see Spier 1917.

3. These mantas are woven by the Hopi men and traded to the Zuni. Traditionally such a handwoven garment was made as a gift to the bride at marriage.

4. See p. 93 for further medical statistics.

5. Parsons 1939: 218. The words transcribed from the Zuni refer to rain and seed fetishes and to fetishes of the Thlewekwe winter society.

6. The author follows the practice of Parsons in her later writing and of Benedict in omitting the tilde over the "n" in Zuni. In pronouncing the common name for their village, the natives do not use the palatalized "n" indicated by the Spanish orthography. In government records and correspondence, the tilde has also been dropped.

7. In Zuni belief, now as in the past, the principal cause of illness and death is witchcraft.

8. Cibola, according to Hodge, was probably a corruption of Ashiwi, the Zuni tribal name, or of the related word, Shiwona, a Zuni name for their country. See Hodge 1937: 12.

9. There is also the possibility, as Hodge points out, that the mission was rebuilt before the Pueblo Revolt in 1680, but if this is true, it was again burned to the ground during the Revolt. Excavation there by the Hodge-Hendricks expedition unearthed only charred beams.

10. The architecture of the parsonage was Dutch colonial, with a steeply-pitched roof which has been the inspiration for some of the Zuni buildings of the early years of this century.

11. Much of Zuni witchcraft belief is quite evidently European derived, but is fused with earlier aboriginal sorcery beliefs and practices. During the periods of Spanish rule, when the religion of the people was endangered, group anxiety must have reached a high pitch and provided an ideal psychological climate for the borrowing of European witchery.

12. Parsons modified this position in her later work. Masks similar in design and type have been excavated in recent years, indicating that masked dances have antecedents dating centuries before the Spanish conquest.

13. See Chapter 8 for date of founding and present enrollment.

14. Because of a careless boundary description of the reservation as it was established in 1877, there was an attempt on the part of General Alexander Logan, acting with several others, to obtain a homestead at Nutria. Had it succeeded, the Zuni would have lost a valuable source of water and some forty farms. The matter was finally settled in 1891 in favor of the Zuni.

15. See Cushing 1920 for the best description of the old agricultural techniques and rituals.

16. It should be noted that all Pueblo warfare was not defensive. The War cult at Zuni, for example, testifies to the former importance of offensive warfare. See Hawley, Patterns of Aggression and the War Cult in Southwestern Pueblos.

17. During a later period in Zuni history, following World War II, several Zuni owned and operated stores. Now, the native storekeeper depends on the craft products of the silversmiths. He has no facilities for buying sheep, which limits the scope of his enterprise.

18. Most of the wheat was grown at Nutria and Pescado and was sold not to traders at Zuni but to traders at Ramah.

19. Many Zuni were employed on construction of this dam. It was through work on the dam and later, in the 1930s, work on the hospital and day school that the Zuni learned to construct with stone and cement mortar, which method they then adapted to the building of their own houses.

20. There are four such officers at Acoma, twenty-one at Laguna, and ten at Isleta. Also see Parsons 1939: 2, 1117, as to the relationship between civil office and irrigator. Parsons also noted the difficulty the Zuni have in carrying out the annual clearing of the irrigation ditches, a project that requires organized effort (Parsons 1917b: 273).

21. The author is indebted to Dr. Laura Thompson for this information (personal communication).

22. Old Jesus, the father of two of the prominent stockmen and exgovernors, is said to have owned at one time over 5,000 sheep and 800 head of cattle.

23. One of the wealthiest stock owners had an income of approximately $17,000 in 1947.

24. This estimate of the population over fourteen years of age is based upon the assumption that the percentage of the total population in that bracket, 65 per cent, was the same in 1947 as it was in 1942, the year in which the United Pueblos Agency computed the population by age groups.

25. In 1940 there were only 138 silversmiths, men and women (see Adair 1944: 198 ff.). The census of silversmiths in 1947 was taken by one of my informants, who used the official tribal census. This he checked with various relatives and friends living in different quarters of the village.

26. It is of interest to note that during the period under consideration a new invention in jewelry technology was made which greatly increased the scope of possible design and was probably in part responsible for the increase in sales. This was the invention of "channeled" turquoise sets, whereby the stones are set in silver cups and the stone and metal are ground down to a flush surface, leaving a pleasing inlay mosaic effect. This technique adapts to a wide range of designs which would have been impossible with the earlier method, whereby round stones were held by separate bezels. Two highly skilled craftsmen lay claim to having made the first jewelry of this type. We may have here a case of multiple invention, but it is unlikely that this is so. More probably there was a single inventor whose work was described by the trader to another smith.

148

27. Although additional data is not available, judging from the above facts, it seems that the women who devoted much of their time to silver work would have considerably less for the time-consuming work in the "waffle gardens." After all, why grow onions if you can buy them? Why grow chili if you can trade silver jewelry to the Isleta farmers in return for a superior variety of pepper?

28. During the war, when "victory garden" campaigns were being promoted all over the country, the farm agent, encouraged by the United Pueblos Agency office, inaugurated a vegetable farming project at Nutria, where the soil and climate is well adapted to truck farming. One farmer made a great success with his cabbage patch and sold several truckloads to Gallup merchants at a good profit. The next year he would not grow a single one. Was he ridiculed by the other farmers for doing women's work? It is likely that public opinion affected his dropping out of the project.

29. It may be surmised that the time spent at silvercraft considerably cuts into the time that used to be spent in the kivas on ceremonial activity. The younger men do not go to the kivas to chat as much as they used to.

30. As Parsons wrote (1917b: 246): "The number of Zuni who work for wages-- for Whites, I have yet to hear of work on such a basis for other Zuni-- is limited (there are five or six wage-earners all told perhaps), but the number is bound to grow."

31. Presumably this was the Jesus family (see footnote 22).

32. General Meeting Held at Zuni Pueblo, February 1943, files, Black Rock.

33. In that same year, during a War Bond drive, five men subscribed over $100 apiece and bought over $500 worth of bonds on this one occasion.

34. Adair 1948, Appendix No. 1. Therein is listed, as of 1947, the clan affiliation of 207 men, all veterans of World War II. The only major difference in size rank, as indicated by this sample of approximately 10 per cent of the population and Kroeber's census of family affiliation by clans, was: Sun clan had dropped from fourth in rank to seventh, Corn clan from sixth to eighth, and Sandhill Crane had advanced from seventh to fourth rank. See Kroeber 1917: 94.

35. These were "phratral groupings" first proposed by Cushing in Outlines of Zuni Creation Myths (1891-92) and later revised in the Handbook of American Indians. Therein (Hodge 1910: 1018): "According to Cushing the Zuni have 7 phratral groups, divided into 16 surviving clans." Also see Kroeber 1917: Table 2.

36. The author has made no detailed study of the problem as Kroeber did, but in reviewing cases that come to mind this association still appears to hold true. It would be of interest to know whether the residents of the farming villages are also included in this clan-directional association, i.e. is Nutria to the north settled by members of the north-oriented clans, Caliente to the south settled by members of the south-oriented clans, etc.?

37. The word is from the Hopi, but it has been used in Pueblo literature to refer to the society of masked dancers in the various pueblos.

38. For a full description and analysis of the Katchina cult see Bunzel 1929-30b.

39. Kluckhohn 1944. See this volume for a similar interpretation of witchcraft in Navaho society.

40. There is only one Bow Priest today.

41. Stevenson (1901-02) says that the governor, the lieutenant governor and all the tenientes were appointed by the Ashiwanni. But she does not say whether this was the case when she was first in the village in 1879. We may surmise, if we accept Cushing's statement, that she is speaking of a later period, possibly when she was in the pueblo during the first years of the present century.

42. The governor's cane, with its large inscribed silver head, is one of those given to the pueblos (except Hopi) by Abraham Lincoln.

43. For the best description of the installation ceremony, see Parsons 1917b: 264 ff.

44. Pro-Catholic and anti-Catholic did not indicate active church going, but sympathy. Nor does anti-Catholic necessarily imply Protestant sympathy. Those who were against the Catholics coming back to Zuni were not necessarily followers of the Dutch Reformed Church.

45. I follow Parsons' spelling. <u>Cíbola</u> is an alternate form.

46. The author is indebted to Omer C. Stewart for the use of his unpublished field notes obtained at Zuni in 1940-41. Much of the material in this chapter is based on these notes.

47. Dr. Laura Thompson has informed the authors in a personal communication that whipping with a strap is a trait of sixteenth- and seventeenth-century Spanish culture which survived to even later times. It spread as a Spanish trait to Guam and may quite possibly be derived from Spain at Zuni as well.

48. I am indebted to Mrs. Margot Astrov for this phrase.

49. Gesell and Ilg 1946. See especially p. 173, "Health and Somatic Complaints."

50. The results for all the tribes on the number of responses, categories used, agreement between raters, and other findings of the tests reported in this chapter, plus the free drawings, may be found in Havighurst and Neugarten 1955.

51. There is an excellent discussion of these two types of social control of the individual in Benedict 1946: chap. 10. See also Piers and Singer 1953.

BIBLIOGRAPHY

Aberle, S. B. D.
  1934   "Maternal Mortality among the Pueblos," American Journal
              of Physical Anthropology," 18, 431-35.

  1948   "The Pueblo Indians of New Mexico: Their Land, Economy,
              and Civil Organization," American Anthropological Associ-
              ation, Memoir, No. 70.

Adair, John
  1944   The Navajo and Pueblo Silversmiths, Norman, University of
              Oklahoma Press.

  1948   "A Study of Culture Resistance: The Veterans of World War
              II at Zuni Pueblo," unpublished Ph.D. dissertation, Univer-
              sity of New Mexico.

Adair, John and E. Vogt
  1949   "Navaho and Zuni Veterans: A Study of Contrasting Modes
              of Culture Change," American Anthropologist, n.s. 51,
              547-61.

Arthur, Mary Grace
  1933   A Point Scale of Performance Tests, 2 vols. New York,
              Commonwealth Fund.

Bavelas, Alex
  1942   "A Method for Investigating Individual and Group Ideologies,"
              Sociometry, 5, 371-77.

Benedict, Ruth
    1934a   Patterns of Culture, Boston, Houghton Mifflin.

    1934b   "Zuni Mythology," Columbia University Contributions to Anthropology, 21, 2 vols. New York.

    1946   The Chrysanthemum and the Sword, Boston, Houghton Mifflin.

Bennett, J. W.
    1946   "The Interpretation of Pueblo Culture: A Question of Values," Southwestern Journal of Anthropology, 2, 361-74.

Bloom, L. B., ed.
    1936   "Bourke on the Southwest," New Mexico Historical Review, 11, 77-122, 188-207.

Bryan, K. and H. F. Robinson
    1928   "Erosion and Sedimentation on the Zuni Watershed, New Mexico," American Geological Society Bulletin, 39, 158-59.

Bunzel, R. L.
    1929   "The Pueblo Potter," Columbia University Contributions to Anthropology, 8, 1-134.

    1929-30a   "Introduction to Zuni Ceremonialism," Forty-seventh Annual Report, Bureau of American Ethnology, pp. 467-544.

    1929-30b   "Zuni Katchinas," Forty-seventh Annual Report, Bureau of American Ethnology, pp. 837-1086.

    1929-30c   "Zuni Origin Myths," Forty-seventh Annual Report, Bureau of American Ethnology, pp. 545-609.

    1929-30d   "Zuni Ritual Poetry," Forty-seventh Annual Report, Bureau of American Ethnology, pp. 611-835.

    1933   "Zuni Texts," Publications of the American Ethnological Society, 15, 1-285.

    1935   "Zuni," in Handbook of American Indian Languages, ed. F. Boas, 4, 389-415.

Bunzel, R. L.
1938   "Economic Organization of Primitive Peoples," in General
            Anthropology, ed. F. Boas, Boston, D. C. Heath.

1940   Lecture notes, Columbia University.

Collier, J.
1947   Indians of the Americas, New York, Mentor.

1949   Patterns and Ceremonials of the Indians of the Southwest,
            New York, E. P. Dutton.

Curtis, E. S.
1926   The North American Indian, 20 vols. Norwood, Mass.,
            Plimpton Press, 17, 85-181.

Cushing, F. H.
1882   "The Zuni Social, Mythic, and Religious Systems," Popular
            Science Monthly, 21, 186-92.

1882-83   "My Adventures in Zuni," Century Magazine, 25, 191-207,
            500-11; 26, 28-47.

1891-92   "Outlines of Zuni Creation Myths," Thirteenth Annual Report,
            Bureau of American Ethnology, pp. 325-447.

1920   "Zuni Breadstuff," Indian Notes and Monographs, Museum of
            the American Indian, Heye Foundation, 8, 7-642.

Dale, E. E.
1949   Indians of the Southwest, Norman, University of Oklahoma
            Press.

Eggan, Fred
1950   Social Organization of the Western Pueblos, Chicago, Uni-
            versity of Chicago Press.

Ellis, F. H.
1951   "Patterns of Aggression and the War Cult in Southwestern
            Pueblos," Southwestern Journal of Anthropology, 7, 177-
            201.

154

Eubank, Lisbeth
1945   "Navaho Mountain Games," El Palacio, Museum of New
         Mexico, Santa Fe.

Ferguson, E.
1931   Dancing Gods, New York, Knopf.

Fuller, C.
1943   "Frank Hamilton Cushing's Relations to Zuni and the
         Hemenway Southwestern Expeditions," unpublished Master's
         thesis, University of New Mexico.

Gesell, Arnold and Frances L. Ilg
1946   The Child from Five to Ten, New York, Harper.

Goldfrank, E.S.
1945   "Socialization, Personality, and the Structure of Pueblo
         Society (With Particular Reference to Hopi and Zuni),"
         American Anthropologist, 47, 516-39.

Goldman, I.
1937   "The Zuni Indians of New Mexico," in Cooperation and
         Competition among Primitive Peoples, ed. M. Mead, New
         York, McGraw-Hill.

Goodenough, Florence L.
1926   Measurements of Intelligence by Drawings, New York, World
         Book Co.

Havighurst, Robert J., Minna K. Gunther, and Inez E. Pratt
1946   "Environment and the Draw-A-Man Test," Journal of Ab-
         normal and Social Psychology, 41, 50-63.

Havighurst, Robert J. and Rhea R. Hilkevitch
1944   "The Intelligence of Indian Children as Measured by a Per-
         formance Scale," Journal of Abnormal and Social Psychology,
         39, 419-33.

Havighurst, Robert J. and Bernice L. Neugarten
1955   American Indian and White Children: A Sociopsychological
         Investigation, Chicago, University of Chicago Press.

155

Hawley, Florence
1948   "Some Factors in the Indian Problems in New Mexico,"
            Publication No. 15, Division of Research, Department of
            Government, University of New Mexico.

n. d.   "Patterns of Aggression and the War Cult in Southwestern
            Pueblos," unpublished manuscript, University of New
            Mexico.

Henry, William E.
1947   The Thematic Apperception Technique in the Study of
            Culture-Personality Relations, Genetic Psychology Mono-
            graphs, No. 35.

Hodge, Frederick Webb
1910   "Zuni," in Handbook of American Indians North of Mexico,
            Bureau of American Ethnology, Bulletin, No. 30, Pt. II,
            pp. 1015-20.

1918   "Excavations at the Zuni Pueblo of Hawikuh in 1917,"
            Art and Archaeology, 7, 367-79.

1923   "Circular Kivas near Hawikuh, New Mexico," Contributions
            from the Museum of the American Indian, Heye Foundation,
            7, No. 1, 1-37.

1937   "History of Hawikuh," Publications of the Frederick Webb
            Hodge Anniversary Publication Fund, Southwest Museum, 1,
            1-155.

1951   "Zuni Witchcraft Again," Masterkey, 25, 7.

Holt, L. E. and Rustin McIntosh
1934   Holt's Diseases of Infancy and Childhood, 10th ed. New York,
            Appleton Century.

Joseph, Alice, Rosamond B. Spicer, and Jane Chesky
1949   The Desert People: A Study of the Papago Indians of Arizona,
            Chicago, University of Chicago Press.

Klopfer, Bruno and D. McG. Kelley
1942   The Rorschach Technique, New York, World Book Company.

156

Kluckhohn, Clyde
1944   Navaho Witchcraft, Papers of the Peabody Museum of
            American Archaeology and Ethnology, Harvard University,
            Vol. 22.

1950   "Conceptions of Death among the Southwestern Indians,"
            Divinity School Bulletin, Harvard University, 66, 5-19.

Kluckhohn, Clyde and Dorothea C. Leighton
1946   The Navaho, Cambridge, Harvard University Press.

Kroeber, A. L.
1916   "The Speech of a Zuni Child," American Anthropologist, n.s.
            18, 529-34.

1917   "Zuni Kin and Clan," Anthropological Papers of the Ameri-
            can Museum of Natural History, 18, Pt. 2, 39-206.

1919   "Zuni," in Encyclopedia of Religion and Ethics, ed. James
            Hastings, 10, New York, Charles Scribners, 868-73.

Leighton, Alexander H. and Dorothea C. Leighton
1949   Gregorio, the Hand-Trembler, Papers of the Peabody Museum
            of American Archaeology and Ethnology, Harvard University,
            Vol. 40.

Leighton, Dorothea C.
1957   "Rorschachs of 87 Zuni Children," in Primary Records in Cul-
            ture and Personality, ed. Bert Kaplan, Microcard Foundation,
            Madison, Wisc., 2, 19.

Leighton, Dorothea C. and Clyde Kluckhohn
1947   Children of the People, Cambridge, Mass., Harvard Univer-
            sity Press.

Li, An-che
1937   "Zuni: Some Observations and Queries," American Anthro-
            pologist, n.s. 39, 62-76.

Macgregor, Gordon
1946   Warriors Without Weapons, Chicago, University of Chicago
            Press.

157

Mills, George
  1947   Field notes.

Mindeleff, V.
  1891   "A Study of Pueblo Architecture, Tusayan and Cibola,"
                Eighth Annual Report, Bureau of American Ethnology, pp.
                13-228.

Mordy, Brooke
  n. d.   "Content Analysis of Indian Children's Drawings: A Method
                for Comparing Culture and Degree of Material Accultura-
                tion," unpublished manuscript, University of Chicago.

Murray, Henry A.
  1938   Explorations in Personality, New York, Oxford University
                Press.

  1943   Thematic Apperception Test Manual, Cambridge, Harvard
                University Press.

Parsons, E.C.
  1915   "Zuni Conception and Pregnancy Beliefs," Proceedings of
                the Nineteenth International Congress of Americanists,
                pp. 378-83.

  1916a   "A Few Zuni Death Beliefs and Practices," American An-
                thropologist, n.s. 18, 245-56.

  1916b   "The Zuni Adoshle and Suuke," American Anthropologist,
                n.s. 18, 338-47.

  1917a   "All-Souls' Day at Zuni, Acoma, and Laguna," Journal of
                American Folklore, 30, 495-96.

  1917b   "Notes on Zuni," Memoirs of the American Anthropological
                Association, 4, 151-327.

  1919-20   "Mothers and Children at Zuni," Man, 19, 168-73.

  1922   "Winter and Summer Dance Series in Zuni in 1918," Uni-
                versity of California Publications in American Archaeology
                and Ethnology, 17, 171-216.

Parsons, E. C.
1924   "The Scalp Ceremonial of Zuni," Memoirs of the American
            Anthropological Association, 31, 1-42.

1927   "Witchcraft among the Pueblos: Indian or Spanish?" Man,
            27, 106-12, 125-28.

1939   Pueblo Indian Religion, University of Chicago Publications
            in Anthropology, Ethnological Series, 2 vols. Chicago, Uni-
            versity of Chicago Press.

Piaget, J.
1929   The Moral Judgment of the Child, New York, Harcourt Brace.

Piers, Gerhart and Milton B. Singer
1953   Shame and Guilt, a Psychoanalytic and a Cultural Study,
            American Lectures in Psychiatry, Publication No. 171,
            Springfield, Ill.

Reed, Erik K.
1949   "Sources of Upper Rio Grande Pueblo Culture and Population,"
            El Palacio, 56, 163-84.

Roberts, F. H. H.
1932   "The Village of the Great Kivas on the Zuni Reservation,"
            Bureau of American Ethnology, Bulletin, No. 111, pp. 1-
            197.

Robinson, E. L., trans.
1944   "Troubles at Zuni in 1702-03," Masterkey, 18, 110-15.

Schneider, D. M. and J. M. Roberts
1956   Zuni Kin Terms, Notebook No. 3, Laboratory of Anthropology,
            University of Nebraska.

Seltzer, Carl C.
1944   Racial Prehistory in the Southwest and the Hawikuh Zunis,
            Papers of the Peabody Museum of American Archaeology and
            Ethnology, Harvard University, 23, 3-37.

Spier, L.
1917   "An Outline for a Chronology of Zuni Ruins," Anthropological
            Papers of the American Museum of Natural History, 18, 207-
            331.

Stevenson, M. C.
    1887   "The Religious Life of the Zuni Child," Fifth Annual Report, Bureau of American Ethnology, pp. 535-55.

    1901-02   "The Zuni Indians: Their Mythology, Esoteric Fraternities, and Ceremonies," Twenty-third Annual Report, Bureau of American Ethnology, pp. 13-608.

Stewart, Kilton R.
    1942   Personal correspondence with Laura Thompson.

Stewart, Omer C.
    1940-41   Field notes.

Thompson, Laura
    1950a   "Action Research among American Indians," Scientific Monthly, 70, 35-40.

    1950b   Culture in Crisis: A Study of the Hopi Indians, New York, Harper.

    1951   Personality and Government: Findings and Recommendations of the Indian Administrative Research, Instituto Indigenista Interamericano, Mexico, D. F.

Thompson, Laura and Alice Joseph
    1944   The Hopi Way, Chicago, University of Chicago Press.

    1946   "White Pressures on Indian Personality and Culture," American Journal of Sociology, 53, 17-22.

Underhill, Ruth M.
    1948   "Ceremonial Patterns in the Greater Southwest," Memoirs of the American Ethnological Society, Vol. 13.

United Pueblos Agency, Office of Indian Affairs, United States Department of the Interior
                Annual Extension Reports, files of the United Pueblos Agency, Albuquerque, New Mexico.

    1931-35   Zuni Subagency, Annual Statistical Reports 1931-35: "Data on Population, Health, Agriculture and Industries," files of the United Pueblos Agency, Albuquerque, New Mexico.

United Pueblos Agency, Office of Indian Affairs, United States Department of
   the Interior

     1941   "Agronomic Report on the Zuni Reservation," unpublished
                 manuscript.

     1946   "Post-war Plan, Zuni Pueblo," unpublished memorandum,
                 files of the United Pueblos Agency, Albuquerque, New
                 Mexico.

Wilson, Edmund
     1949   "Shalako," New Yorker, 25, No. 7, 62-73; No. 8, 70-82.

Woodward, Arthur
     1950   "Concerning Witches," Masterkey, 24, 183-88.

Woodbury, R. B.
     1956   "The Antecedents of Zuni Culture," Transactions of the
                 New York Academy of Sciences, 18, 557-63.

INDEX

Aberle, Sophie, 58, 59
Acculturation, 77, 116,
    118, 143
Achievement, 101-02,
    103-04
Acoma, 13, 15, 147
Adair, John, v, vi
Adolescence, 74-77
Agemates, 105-06, 123
Aggression, 98-104, 108-11,
    118-19, 140-42
Aggressiveness, Zuni dislike
    for, 123, 140
Agricultural Adjustment Ad-
    ministration, 28
Agriculture, 21-22, 117; im-
    plements of, 23, 28; income
    from, 34; production, 30, 34;
    and religion, 23, 27-29, 45-
    47; skills, 13
Ahayuta, 50
Albuquerque, 8, 87; Indian
    School at, 80
Amusements, 97-98, 108-11, 122
Amy, 124-26, 139
Analysis of tests, 83-84
Anasazi, 13, 45; culture, 14
Angela, 132-35, 139, 143;
    autobiography of, 133-35
Anger, 74, 123, 141; in
    Emotional Response test, 96,
    100, 105

Anglo-American settlers, 13
Annual Extension Reports, United
    Pueblos Agency, 28, 29, 30
Apache, 13, 18, 23; raids, 19-20,
    21; Zuni wars with, 55
"Apollonian" behavior, 72-74, 140-
    42
Appearance, 6, 8, 94, 140
Arthur, Grace, Point Performance
    scale, 80, 81, 83, 85-86, 88-90,
    125, 127, 130, 131, 135, 138
Arts and crafts, 123
Ashiwanni, 41, 43, 48, 55, 149
"Ashiwi," 12, 145
Associated persons, relationships to, 95
Astrov, Mrs. Margot, 150
Athabaskans, 13, 23
Atoshle, 68, 77
Atsinna, 14, 15
Authority, 118; see also Control,
    Discipline
Automobiles, 9, 77, 141
Avila y Ayala, Pedro de, 18

Background material, for testing, 80-81
Badger clan, 40
Barnett, Clifford, vii
"Basketmakers," 45
Bavelas, Alex, 81; Moral Ideology
    test, 107-11
Beadwork, 26, 66
Bear (god), 46

162

Beast Gods, 45, 46, 51
Behavior, 101-02; "Apollonian,"
  72-74, 140-42; "Dionysian,"
  141; individual, 64, 118, 139;
  rules of, 74; social, 88-90
Benedict, Ruth, 74, 140-41, 145;
  Patterns of Culture, 72-74
Best thing, reaction to, in Emo-
  tional Response test, 96, 102,
  105
Birnbaum, Richard, 80
Black Rock, 5, 9-10, 31; boarding
  school at, 87; hospital at, 62;
  subagency at, 10, 22, 26
Black Rock Dam, 5, 26
Black Rock Reservoir, 9
Blame, 109-11, 123; in Moral
  Ideology test, 109-11
Boarding schools, 87, 88
Bourke, Captain John, 24, 26
Bow Priests, 48-49, 50, 52, 55,
  57, 77, 143, 149; Elder Brother,
  50; Younger Brother, 50
Bunker, Robert, vii
Bunker, Mrs. Robert, vii
Bunzel, Ruth, 11-12, 31, 36, 45,
  48-49, 57, 71; "Zuni Origin
  Myths," 12
Burial customs, 78-79
Burros, 23

Caciques, 18, 37
Cane, governor's, 51, 56, 149
Cash economy, see Economy
Casteñeda, 17
Catholic Church, 19-20, 22, 56, 87,
  149; mission school, 84
Cattle, 23, 31; ownership of, 31;
  see also Livestock
Ceremonial designs, in free drawings,
  82; in Rorschach test, 115
Ceremonial life, 43, 118-19, 123

Ceremonials, group, 45-48, 54,
  142, 144, 148; installation, 149;
  revival of, 52; as source of happi-
  ness, 97-98; see also Dances,
  Rituals
Chaco Canyon, 14
Change, acceptance of, 3; in civil
  government, 34; economic, 21-25,
  34-38, 59; in morals, 76-77;
  motivation for, 29-30; religious,
  34, 52-54; resistance to, 3, 27-
  29; of rules, 113; social, 59;
  in values, 34-38, 53-54, 59
Chaperonage, 77
Charles, 126-27, 139
Chesky, Jane, The Desert People, v
Child behavior, vi
Child care, vi, 61, 62-74; in infancy,
  62-64
Child development, vi
Child training, see Training
Childbirth, 60-62
Children, Zuni, 122-44
Children of the People, Kluckhohn and
  Leighton, v
Children of the Sun, 11-12
Chili peppers, 21
Christian Church, influence of, 20-21;
  and state, 55-59
Christian Reformed Church, 11, 20,
  87; mission school, 84, 87, 88
Cibola, 15-17, 18, 145, 150
Civil government, 21, 55-59; changes
  in, 34; difficulties of, 59; rise of,
  37-38
Clans, 12, 40-41, 142, 148; Badger,
  40; Corn, 148; Deer, 40; Dogwood,
  40; function of, 39, 61; matrilineal,
  39-41; Sandhill Crane, 148; struc-
  ture of, 39-41; Sun, 148
Clara, 127-30, 139, 143; autobiography of, 127-28

Classic Period (Pueblo III), 14
Climate, 5-6
Clinics, 92
Collier, John, 10, 26-27
Colorado plateau, 4, 13
Committee on Human Develop-
ment, University of Chicago,
v, 80, 81, 83
Communication, 9
Conflict, between generations,
77; political, 58-59, 142
Conformity, 88-90, 120, 122-
23, 124, 138; in intelligence
levels, 88-90; in social be-
havior, 88-90; in values, 88-
90
Conquistadores, 10, 15
Conscience, 111
Continental Divide, 6
Control, 119; religious, 47;
weather, 23, 45, 54; see
also Authority, Discipline
Cooperation, 37
Corn, 12-13, 23, 117; see also
Agriculture, Crops
Corn clan, 148
Corn Mountain, 5
Coronado, 14-17
Council of priests, 55, 57-58
Courtship, 77
Cousins, 42
Cradleboard, 62
Cremation, 15
Crops, 21, 23, 27-31, 53, 140;
ownership of, 30-31; total
worth, 28-29; see also Agri-
culture
Crow system, 42
Cult, 48-52; of the Beast Gods, 51,
142; of the Katchina Priests, 49;
of the Sun, 48-49; of the War
Gods, 50

Cultural traits, 138
Culture (Zuni), vi, 116-17, 119,
138-39, 140; see also White
culture
Curers, 45-46, 53-54, 144
Curing societies, 51, 52, 54, 60,
141-42
Cushing, F. H., 25, 50, 55; "My
Adventures in Zuni," 24; Outlines
of Zuni Creation Myths, 149;
"Zuni Breadstuffs," 146

Dances, ceremonial, 36, 46-54, 69-
71; see also Ceremonials, Rituals
Danger, 98-99
Death, 98, 103-04, 145; customs,
20, 78-79; and witchcraft, 78
Deatherage, Marie, 80
Deer clan, 40
Delinquency, 99
Descent, 30-31, 42
Desert People, The, Alice Joseph,
Rosamond Spicer, and Jane Chesky, v
Detail, attention to, 90, 120
Diego de Vargas, 18-19
Diet, 24, 35; of children, 64-65; in
pregnancy, 60
Disappointment, 98
Discipline, 47, 71, 98-99, 100-04,
118-19; of adolescents, 74-77; of
children, 67-68, 71; see also
Authority, Control
Diseases, contagious, 78; most preva-
lent, 91-94; skin, 91-94; venereal,
91-94
Division of labor, 30-32
Division of ownership, see Ownership
Divorce, 78
Dogwood clan, 40
Dress, 2, 6, 8
Drinking, 77, 108-11, 142

Dutch Reformed Church, 20, 149; see also Christian Reformed Church
Dwellings, 2, 13
Dysentery, 91-92

Economy, 117, 143; cash, 35-38; changes in, 21-22, 23-25, 34-38, 59; growth of, 58-59; importance of sheep in, 32-33
Education, 87-88; see also Schools
Eggan, Fred, Social Organization of the Western Pueblos, 42
Elder Brother, see Bow Priests
Ellis, Florence Hawley, viii
Embarrassment, 100-01, 103-04, 123, 140
Emotional Response test, 64, 95, 96-107; see also Anger, Best thing, Fear, Happiness, Sadness, Shame, Worst thing
English language, 2, 9, 12, 80-82, 85, 95, 104, 111, 124, 126, 142
Erickson, Mrs. Kathleen, 80
Erosion, 6, 25, 32
Estevan, 16, 18
Ettowe, 40, 44, 46, 47
European influence, 17

Family, 111, 118, 122-23; extended, 139; of procreation, 31; relationships, 105-06; solidarity, 97-98, 101-02, 107-11
Farm Extension, 27-30
Farming, 23-38, 123; see also Agriculture
Father, 105-06, 118
Fear, 123; feelings of, in the Emotional Response test, 96, 99, 105; of the supernatural, 63-64, 103-04
Fertility, 42; worship, 23

Fetishes, 40, 41, 44, 55, 56, 145
Firearms, 23
Food, ownership of, 94
Franciscans, see Missionaries, Missions
Francisco Letrado, Fray, 18
Francisco de la Madre de Dios, Fray, 18
Frank, 135-38, 139, 143; autobiography of, 136-38
Fred Harvey Company, 25
Free drawings, 82, 115-17; analysis of, 115; method of collecting, 115-16

Gallup, 1, 9, 141, 143
Games, 67; see also Recreation, Rules of games
Gods, 45-48; see also Bear (god), Beast Gods, War Gods
Goldman, I., 72
Gonzales, Mr., vii
Gonzales, Mrs. Clara, vii, 80, 81, 82, 95, 124
Goodenough Draw-A-Man test, 81, 85-86, 88-90, 125, 127, 130, 131, 135
Gossip, 72-73, 119, 141
Government, checks, 34, 36; day school, 84-85, 87, 88; workers, 56, 141
Governor, 51, 55-59, 149
Graham, Douglas, 24, 26

Halona(wa), 17, 18, 19
Handbook of American Indians, F. W. Hodge, 149
Happiness, feelings of, in Emotional Response test, 96-98, 105
Harvest Dance, 36
Hassrick, Royal, 83
Havighurst, Robert J., 83
Hawikuh, 5, 15, 16-17, 18, 19, 21

Health, of Zuni children, 91-94
Height, 93-94
Henry, William E., 83, 117
Hepatina (Middle Place), 11-12
Herding, 23-38, 66, 123
History, 10, 11-22; archaeological, 13-15; mythological, 11-13
Hodge, Frederick Webb, 15, 145, 146; Handbook of American Indians, 149
Hodge-Hendricks expedition, 146
Hohokam, 15
Hollonawa (Ant Place), 12
Homogeneity, 138
Hopi, 6, 13, 22, 24, 27, 39, 40, 43, 49, 78, 103-04, 114, 117, 118, 140, 142, 149; influence, 19; land use, 4; raids, 19; reservation, 5
Hopi Way, The, Laura Thompson and Alice Joseph, v
Horses, 23-24
Hotevilla, 142
Household, 40
Howard, Josephine, 80, 81

Illness, 98, 145; see also Diseases
Imagination, 119, 123
Immanent justice and animism, test of, 95, 111-12
Impeachment, of governor, 58
Implements, agricultural, 23, 28
Income, 33-34; tax, 36
Indian administration, v
Indian agency, at Black Rock, 10, 22, 26
Indian Education Research Project, v, vi, 80
Indian Service, 22, 25, 26, 37, 53, 57, 58

Individual, anxiety of, 54, 142; behavior, 64, 118, 139; life cycle of, 60-79; morality, 109; relation of, to clan, 40-41; religious needs of, 46-48; variations, 120, 124, 144
Infancy, 62-64; mortality in, 91
Initiation ceremonies, 68-71
Innovation, see Change
Intelligence, 123; conformity in, 88-90; quota (IQ), mean, 88-90; sex differences in, 90; tests, 81-90; of Zuni children, 81, 87-90
Interpersonal relationships, 118-19, 123, 140
Interpreters, 81, 82
Interviewing, 80-81
IQ, see Intelligence
Irrigation, 4, 13, 21-22, 26-27
Isleta, 34, 54, 147, 148
Itiwani, 12
Itiwawa (Middle Place), 12

Jesus, Old, 147; family of, 148
Jewelry, 8, 25-26, 53; see also Silvercraft
Joseph, Alice, 83; The Desert People, v; The Hopi Way, v
Juan Galdo, Fray, 18

Kakwemosi, 48, 57
Kaplan, Bert, viii
Katchina (ancestors), 140; cult or society of, 21, 40, 41, 43, 49, 52, 68-71, 149; dancers, 53, 78, 79; Priests, 51, 54; scare, 68; Village, 79
Kechipawan, 17
Kelley, D. McG., and Bruno Klopfer, The Rorschach Technique, 119
Kelsey, Charles, 24

K'iakima, 17
Kinship, 40, 42-44
Kiva, 2, 14, 49, 61, 69,
    140, 148; groups, 51,
    52, 142
Klopfer, Bruno, 83; and D.
    McG. Kelley, The Rorschach
    Technique, 119
Kluckhohn, Clyde, viii; Chil-
    dren of the People, v; The
    Navaho, v
Kok'okshi, 12
Koluwala·wa, 71
Kotikan·e, 40
Koyemshi, 12, 50-51
Kroeber, A. L., 39-44, 52, 148,
    149; "Zuni Kin and Clan," 39-
    44
Kwakina, 17
Kwilliyallane, 5

Labor, 30-32
Laguna, 3, 32, 34, 54, 59, 147
Lamy, Bishop, 20
Land, ownership of, 30-31; use,
    4, 22
Language, bad, 108-11; diffi-
    culty with, 95; Navaho, 8;
    Spanish, 9; Zunian, 8-9, 12,
    112; see also English language
Las Cruces, 29
Legends, 11-13
Leighton, Alexander H., viii
Leighton, Dorothea, v, vi, 80, 83,
    124; Children of the People, v;
    The Navaho, v
Lerner, Eugene, 112
Lieutenant governor, 55, 56, 57,
    58, 59, 149
Life cycle, see Individual
Lincoln, Abraham, 149
Lineages, 40, 41, 42-43; function
    of, at birth, 60-61

Livestock, 21, 23, 30-33; in-
    come from, 30, 34; introduc-
    tion of, 23; production, 36
Logan, General Alexander, 146
Loss, of friends or family, 98
Lying-in period, 61-62

Macgregor, Gordon, Warriors with-
    out Weapons, v
Marcos de Niza, Fray, 15-16
Marriage, 77-78; and clan, 39;
    endogamous, 39
Masks, 146, 149
Material culture, 2; see also Cul-
    tural traits, Culture (Zuni)
Material possessions, 44
Maternal mortality, 91-93
Matriarchal system, 94
Matrilineal lineage, 30-31, 40; see
    also Lineages
Matrilocal residence, 44
Matsaki, 17
Mayordomos, 27
Medical care, 10, 92
Medical examinations, see Physical
    examinations
"Medicine, general," 51
Medicine men, 92; see also Curers
Medicine societies, 52; see also
    Curing societies
Mendoza, 15-17
Menstruation, 74-75
Mesa Verde, 14
Messengers of the Gods, see Shalako
Mexican origin legend, 12
Meyer, Adolf, vii
Middle Place, 2, 11, 144; People
    of the, 79
Mills, George, viii
Missionaries, 53, 56, 84-85, 141;
    Franciscan, 18-20
Missions, 20, 22, 56, 146; Franciscan,
    18-20; see also Catholic Church

Modernization, at Zuni, 9-10
Moral Ideology test, 95, 105,
 107-11
Morality, 108-12; individual,
 109; rules of, 111-12; sexual,
 108-11; social, 109
Morals, changing, 76-77
Mortality rate, 91-92
Mother, 105-06, 118
Motivation, for change, 29-30
Murray, Henry A., 82, 83
Mutual obligation, 31
Mythology, 10, 11-13

Navaho, 8, 13, 22, 23, 24, 25,
 51, 66, 77, 101, 104, 114,
 117, 140, 149; children, 87;
 raids, 19-20; Zuni wars with,
 55
Navaho, The, Clyde Kluckhohn and
 Dorothea Leighton, v
Negative relationships, see Inter-
 personal relationships
Nominating committee, 56-58
Nursing, 64
Nutria, 5, 14, 27, 57, 146, 149;
 Creek, 4-5; valley, 26

Offerings, to the gods, 47
Ojo Caliente, 5, 9, 26, 57, 149
Olson, Walter, vii
Oraibi, 15, 142
Origin legends, 11-13
Outlines of Zuni Creation Myths,
 F. H. Cushing, 149
Outsiders, 123
Ownership, 30-31; of cattle, 30-
 31; of crops, 30-31; of food,
 94; of land, 30-31; of sheep,
 31; by women, 30-31
Oxen, 23-24

Papago, 101, 104, 114, 117, 140
Parasites, 91-94
Parents, 123
Parsons, Elsie Clews, 20-21, 52, 56,
 68, 140, 145, 146, 147, 150;
 Pueblo Indian Religion, 11-12
Paternalism, 58
Patrilocal residence, 44
Patterns of Culture, R. Benedict, 72-
 74
Peach trees, 21
Pekwin (Sun Priest), 48-49, 52, 55,
 58, 143
Personality, vi, 141; development
 of, v; traits, 138, 139
Personality and Government, Laura
 Thompson, v
Pescado, 5, 27, 57, 146
Peter, 130-32
"Phratral groupings," 149
Physical appearance, see Appearance
Physical examinations, 80, 81, 90-94
Piaget, Jean, 81, 111-12
Political conflicts, 58-59, 142
Popé, 18
Population, 6; growth of, 6, 7
Positive relationships, see Interpersonal
 relationships
Pottery making, 13 ff., 66
Power system, 37-38
Praise, 109-11, 123
Prayer stick, 47
Prayers, 47-48; see also Rituals
Pregnancy, 60, 75
Presbyterian mission school, 87
Priest of the North, 40, 48, 57
Priest of the South, 40
Priests, 37, 40, 45, 141; see also Bow
 Priests, Katchina Priests, Pekwin
 (Sun Priest), Priest of the North,
 Priest of the South, Rain Priests

Principales, 59
Projective tests, 82, 115-21
Property, 97-98, 100, 101-02;
    and possessions, as source of hap-
    piness, 97-98, 103-04, 122
Protestant church, 56, 149; mis-
    sions, 20, 22
Psychological battery, 79, 81, 95-
    114; see also Emotional Response
    test, Immanent justice and ani-
    mism, Moral Ideology test,
    Rules of games
Puberty, 74-75
Public health, 10
Pueblo culture, 13, 47, 117; con-
    tinuity of, 140-41; development
    of, 13-15; and religion, 45;
    training of boys in, 90
Pueblo III (Classic Period), 14
Pueblo Indian Religion, E.C.
    Parsons, 11-12
Pueblo Indians, administration
    of, 26
Pueblo Revolt, 18-19, 146
Purification, 47

Railroads, 24, 25
Rain, 117, 144
Rain Priests, 40, 41, 48, 56
Ramah, 5, 146; Navaho, 10;
    see also Navaho
Recreation, 66-67
Relationships, personal, in Emo-
    tional Response test, 104-07;
    of Zuni child to agemates,
    others, parents, siblings, 95;
    see also Interpersonal relation-
    ships
Religion, 14, 20-21, 144; and
    agriculture, 23, 27-29; changes
    in, 34, 52-55; force of, 2; nega-
    tive aspects of, 54; observance of,

108-11, 117, 122; Pueblo, 20, 45;
    purpose and functions, 45-47; sanc-
    tions, 28, 35; structure of, 48-52;
    techniques of, 47-48; traditional,
    38; see also Rituals
Reservation (Zuni), 4-6
Residence, 41, 44
Responses, to Emotional Response test,
    96-97
Restrictions, during pregnancy, 60
Ridicule, sensitivity to, 29, 72, 140-
    42
Rio Grande pueblos, 6, 13, 27, 59
Rio Grande river, 16; valley, 17
Rio Nutria, 5
Rio Pescado, 5
Rituals, 45-55, 71; and agriculture,
    140; at birth, 61; curing, 53;
    formulas, 45-48; group, 45, 141-
    42; war, 50; see also Ceremonials,
    Dances, Religion
Roads, 9
Roberts, Frank, 14
Roberts, John, viii, 42
Rodriguez-Chamuscado expedition, 17
Rodriguez Cubero, Pedro, 19
Roque de Figueredo, 18
Rorschach Technique, The, B. Klopfer
    and D. Kelley, 119
Rorschach test, 46, 80, 82, 85-86,
    115, 119-21, 125, 127, 130-31,
    135, 138; analysis of, 83
Rules of games, test of attitudes toward,
    95, 112-14

Sadness, in Emotional Response test,
    96, 98-99, 105
Safety valves, 142
St. Anthony's Mission School, 87, 88
San Juan, 14; river, 15
Sanitation, 91-92
Santa Clara, 54

Santa Fe, 8, 26, 80, 87
Scalp Dance, 52, 53
Scaring, as discipline, 71
Schneider, David M., 42
Schools, 84-85, 87-88, 108-11,
122; public, 84-85
Scolding, as discipline, 67, 71
Secrecy, 48; religious, 50, 55
Secularization, 53, 54, 59
Selection of subjects, in testing
program, 84-86
Self-gratification, 103-04
Sensitivity, 140-41, 142; see
also Ridicule
Sex differences, in IQ, 90
Sexual relations, 67, 123; con-
trol in 120-21; and morality,
108-11; premarital, 75-77
Shalako (ceremony), 30, 36,
37, 48-52, 57, 129, 144
Shalako (Messengers of the Gods),
11, 49-51
Shamans, 45, 54, 142
Shame, 123, 140, 144; in Emo-
tional Response test, 96, 100-
01, 105; as means of discipline,
72; in Zuni culture, 107
Sheep, 31-33, 117, 146; camps,
31-32; management of, 31-32;
ownership of, 31
Shiwanakwe (Middle Place), 12
Shiwanni, 57
Shiwona, 145
Siblings, 42, 105-06
Sichomovi, 19
Sickness, see Illness
Silvercraft, 25-38, 146-48; in-
come from, 33-34
Sioux, 77, 84, 101, 103-04, 114,
117, 118, 140
Sipaloa, 57
Skin diseases, 91-94

Social control, 109, 118, 140,
143; of behavior, 88-90;
methods of, 2, 72
Social organization, 15, 60; changes
in, 43-44; Pueblo, 20; traditional,
38
Social Organization of the Western
Pueblos, Fred Eggan, 42
Spanish, authorities, 55; colonies,
13; Conquest, 15-17; culture,
150; history, 10; influence, 20-
21, 23
Spicer, Rosamond, The Desert Peo-
ple, v
Sports, 67; see also Games, Recrea-
tion
Stealing, 108-11
Stevenson, M. C., 24, 87, 149
Stewart, Kilton, 96
Stewart, Omer C., vi, viii, 150
Stock, improvement program, 32;
reduction program, 22, 25, 32-33,
142; see also Livestock
Structure, of religious organization,
48-52; see also Religion
Subsistence farming, 30; see also
Farming
Sun Priest, see Pekwin
Supernatural, 43, 46, 98-99, 105-
06, 123; and agriculture, 29, 45-
47; fear of, 103-04; reliance on,
29; threats of, 71; see also
Witches and witchcraft

Taboos, 47
Taos, 13
Tapup, 57
TAT, see Thematic Apperception test
Teachers, 84-85, 105-06, 141
Technological advances, 142
Tekapa (Hill Ranch), 5
Telephones, 9

Temperature, 6
Tenientes, 27, 55, 56, 59, 149
Tension, 142-43
Testing program, at Zuni, v-vi, 80, 139; analysis in, 83-84; meaning of, 84; selection of subjects for, 84-86
Textiles, 24
Thematic Apperception test (TAT), 80, 82, 83, 85-86, 115, 117-19, 125, 127, 130, 131, 135, 138
Thlewekwe winter society, 145
Thompson, Laura, viii, 147, 150; The Hopi Way, v; Personality and Government, vi
Thoughtfulness, 108-11
Threats, as discipline, 71
Thunder Mountain, 5
Toilet training, 65
Tourists, 25
Toyallane (Toyallene), 5, 16-19
Trachoma, 92
Trade, 24, 35
Traders, 9-10, 22, 37, 56, 85, 141; and trading posts, 24-25, 31
Training, of children, 65-74, 103-04, 106-07; household, 66; moral, 110; toilet, 65
Travel, as source of happiness, 97-98
Trees, planting of, 21, 27-28
Tuberculosis, 91-94
Turquoise, 26, 46; see also Jewelry, Silvercraft

Undernutrition, 93
United Pueblo Service, 22
United Pueblos Agency, vii, 7, 10, 32, 58, 148; Annual Extension Reports, 28, 29, 30
United States government, 22
United States Office of Indian Affairs, v
Uwanami, 143

Values, 3; changes in, 34-38, 53-54, 59; conformity in, 88-90; traditional, 59
Vanderwagen Brothers, 24
Venereal disease, 91-94
Veterans, of World War II, vi, vii, 6, 28, 29, 52, 72, 142, 148
Veteran's Administration, 28, 35-36
Vogt, Evon, vii

"Waffle gardens," 21, 27, 148
Wages, for herding, 32
Wallace, C. G., 24
War cult, 48, 52, 53, 55, 146
War Gods, 2, 50
Warfare, 50, 146; rituals of, 50
Warriors without Weapons, Gordon Macgregor, v
Water resources, 9, 26-27
Weaning, 64
Weather control, 23, 45, 54
Weight, 93-94
Weinrich, Mrs. Marcel, vii
Wheat, 23, 146
Whipping, 47, 69-72, 141, 150
White children, intelligence of, 88-90, 123; testing of, 103-04, 112
White culture, 87, 116-18, 120, 123, 140, 143
Whites, at Zuni, 9
Whithorn, John C., vii
Witches and witchcraft, 20, 47, 50, 51, 53-54, 61, 72-74, 79, 98-99, 108-11, 141-43, 145-46; as cause of death, 78; Navaho, 149;

protection from, 63-64; see also Supernatural
Wittfogel, Esther Goldfrank, viii
Women, ownership by, 30-31
Woodbury, Richard, 14-15
Wool, 32
Work, in Moral Ideology test, 107-11, 122, 139
Worst thing, reaction to, in Emotional Response test, 96, 102, 105

Younger Brother, see Bow Priests

Zia, 103-04, 114, 117, 140
"Zuni child," the, 122-24
Zuni mountains, 4-5
Zuni (pueblo), description of, 1-7; origin of, 19
Zuni river, 4
Zunian (language), 8-9, 12, 112

DERAL INDIAN RESERVATIONS AND HEALTH FACILITIES
UNDER THE JURISDICTION OF THE ALBUQUERQUE AREA OFFICE
(Arizona, Colorado, New Mexico, Utah)

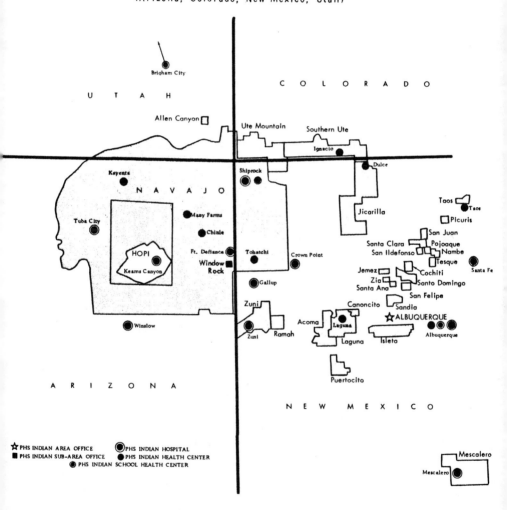

1. The old terraced pueblo, about 1897

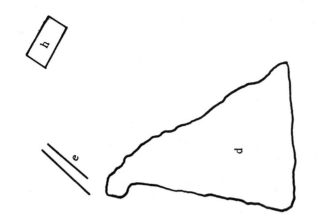

2. Aerial view of Zuni, 1947

   a. Old Catholic Mission
   b. Graveyard
   c. Dance Plaza
   d. Chili gardens
   e. Bridge over Zuni river
   f. Christian Reformed Church and School
   g. Vanderwagon's trading post
   h. Kelsey's trading post.

3. Zuni pueblo with Toyallene, the sacred mesa, in the background

4. Zuni and Toyallene in winter

5. The central dance plaza

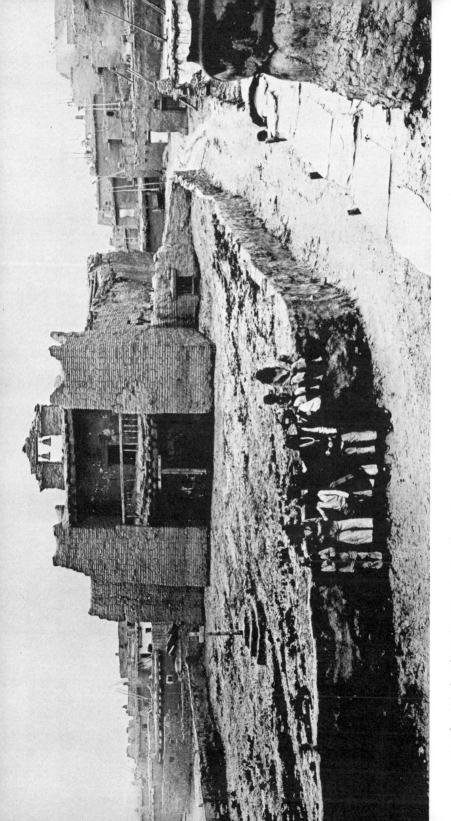

6. The old church in the late nineteenth century

7. An ancient spring

8. A vegetable garden

9. Building an oven

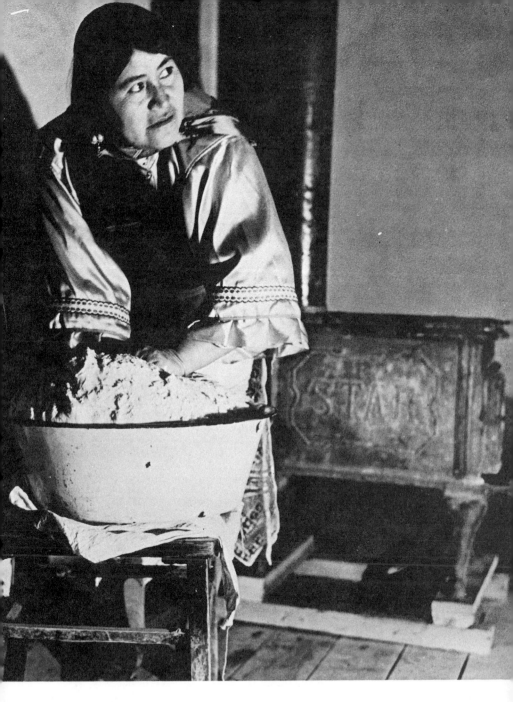

10. Bread dough is prepared in large quantities

11. Baking bread for several families

12. Enough dough for an oven-full

13. A full oven

14. Some of the grazing land is bare and eroded

15. Lambs penned for selling

16. Splitting firewood

17. Drawing water from the village well

18. Silversmith carving a rock mold

19. Grinding corn in the ancient way with <u>metate</u> and <u>mano</u>

20. An old Zuni potter, 1940

21. A woman silversmith

22. Men in black blankets, 1940

23. Schoolgirls with shawls

24. Zuni schoolgirls

25. Ready for a cere-
    monial dance

27. An old woman of the Badger clan

26. A middle-aged woman

28. A Zuni housewife

29. A Zuni woman with her basket of ceremonial cornmeal

30. A fortune in turquoise

31. A young Zuni couple